WHILE I'M ON MY FEET

WHILE
I'M ON MY FEET

Gerald Kennedy

ABINGDON PRESS / New York • Nashville

WHILE I'M ON MY FEET

Copyright © 1963 by Abingdon Press

Library of Congress Catalog Card Number: 63-8668

SET UP, PRINTED, AND BOUND BY THE
PARTHENON PRESS, AT NASHVILLE,
TENNESSEE, UNITED STATES OF AMERICA

This is for Mary

PREFACE

I have tried to find some reason for writing this book that would justify my efforts. But so far as making its appearance of unusual significance is concerned, all the reasons I have come up with have sounded unconvincing even to me. My experiences have not been so unique as to make their telling an end in itself. I have no special wisdom about either the past or the future. There is no lectureship involved demanding publication.

It comes down to the simple fact that I thought it would be enjoyable to reminisce and give my personal opinion on a number of things. I expect that the factor which nearly always shapes our opinions—though we are loath to confess it—is our personal experiences. When a man says, "That is not true," or "I disagree," he is saying that his experiences do not lead to such conclusions. Thus, human backgrounds are always of real interest to me, and perhaps they are to others.

So far as the ministry is concerned, we are likely to allow certain personal experiences with individuals to influence us too much. It is only when we view our life and work from the perspective of thirty years or so, that we begin to see things in proportion. Such a testimony from any man may be of help to young men. I hope so.

This has been more fun writing than anything else I have done. Such a feeling in itself makes me suspicious of the results. My thanks go to Abingdon Press for counsel and to my secretary, Mrs. Dorothy Hancock, for carrying an extra burden without complaint. My wife, as usual, wielded a red pencil with her usual encouragement, skill, and good judgment.

—GERALD KENNEDY

CONTENTS

I APPRECIATE THE HONOR . . .

THIS GREAT RESPONSIBILITY . . .

LET ME BE FRANK . . .

I PROCLAIM WITHOUT FEAR . . .

CONSIDER WITH ME . . .

Contents

SITUATION

As I have tried to set the stage for what follows, the opening line of Edward Rowland Sill's *Opportunity* keeps ringing in my mind:

This I beheld, or dreamed it in a dream:—

There was a meeting of a large committee appointed to study the ministry and especially the episcopacy. I came in late and sat in the back of the auditorium. There was much personal testimony by ministers, too much reminiscing, too few facts, and too many broad conclusions. But I listened with patience.

Finally the chairman, who was a most courteous brother, being duly informed by some fellow that I was present, called my name.

"Bishop," he asked, "is there anything you would care to add?"

"No," I replied with just the right note of indecisiveness, "I think not. The subject seems to have been covered quite adequately." This is the way a man is expected to reply to such a question.

"But"—and this is always the counterpoint to the negative beginning—"WHILE I'M ON MY FEET, I would like to say a few words."

UNACCUSTOMED
AS I AM...

BACKGROUND   There are very few people who know less about their family background than I know about mine. My father was a rolling stone who never stayed anywhere long enough to gather moss or much of anything else. The longest we ever lived in one city was six years, and we moved four times during that period. We came to California from Michigan when I was five years old and the bonds with the past were severed completely. I have some uncles and cousins in the West, but we have not kept up our correspondence.

My mother was born in Vermont, and an old gentleman once told me that her father was remembered for his blunt, salty, and forthright speech. The old gentleman thought I might have inherited some of his qualities. My father's family came down from Canada and some-body told me once that originally they were from the north of Ireland. My father was a local preacher in The Methodist Church and a man who knew very little contentment or peace of mind. Hampered by lack of formal education, he could never adjust himself to the gap be-tween what he wanted to do and what he was able to do. He was the victim of frustration and sickness.

I think this rootlessness has influenced my life and point of view. When I entered high school, some of my friends who came from good families simply assumed a security and status I never knew. There was a period when I took my lunch away from the school and ate it under an old railroad trestle. This was one of those behavior patterns of adolescence that are so ridiculous to everyone but the adolescent. It was a period of loneliness, bashfulness, withdrawal. At least it saved me from the nostalgia for childhood that haunts so many people, and it gave me a great sympathy for every lonely child.

Things changed suddenly when we moved to a new town and I made a speech in a high-school assembly. A great public-speaking teacher influenced my life by opening up opportunities for speaking contests and debating. I was elected president of the student body and became one of the student leaders. Oscar Levant once said that if a kid could not play baseball, he had no choice but to become a concert pianist. My work after school and in the morning prevented athletics except sporadically, and so there was no choice but to speak. And at last I belonged.

Our public school system may have changed since my day, but I remember high school as the most democratic society I have ever known. The difference in social status did not matter and the wealth of one's parents had nothing to do with student prestige. Some rich boys were liked and some were not. Some poor boys were given honors and some were not. So far as I could see, each student stood on his own feet and was judged by his own life.

Those who attack the American public school system cannot be aware of what this foundation of our civilization means. Imagine a generation divided into sectarian, parochial schools and ask if such an eventuality would not spell disaster. I know all the vaunted advantages that are supposed to come from private schools. But for America, the public school system is one of the essentials. We do not all go to the same church, nor should we; but it is important that most of us should be thrown together in a common educational experience. I have never heard it proposed seriously that an American high school is a substitute for family background, but it worked out that way for me.

I am not much impressed by biographies that spend a long chapter tracing a man's ancestry back before the Middle Ages. That may be of some academic interest, but it is of no real importance in understanding the man himself. Take a quick look at a fellow's parents and go back to his grandparents if you must, but that is far enough. Beyond that point blood flows in too many directions from too many sources.

No, the important thing is what family a person chooses for himself. Where does he feel at home? Whom does he accept as his models and his companions? Which environment does he enter? Jesus' rather abrupt word to his own family expresses the situation perfectly. It is true always that my real family are those whose will and purposes are my own. And so gradually I have overcome my sense of awe when I meet people of famous ancestry, and I am making some progress in overcoming my own feeling of inferiority because my father was not what we would call a success.

My family has been more and more The Methodist Church. I am a spiritual son of John Wesley. I do not say that I could not have been happy and at ease in another communion, but this one fits me best. Theoretically I can believe that another woman might have been a satisfactory wife, but practically I do not believe it at all. There was only one in the world for me and the good Lord led me to her. Likewise, I am a natural-born Wesleyan and it was predestined that I should be a Methodist. This is mixing the theologies somewhat, but a little mixing is good for them.

My whole life has been centered in the church. I went to church in my mother's arms and slept on the back seat while my father was finishing his Sunday-evening sermons. I never missed Sunday school and I was a member of the Epworth League. It seemed inevitable to me that the ministry was my calling for as long ago as I can remember. That beautiful prayer, *For the Church,* says it perfectly:

We remember with love the nurture she gave to our spiritual life in its infancy, the tasks she set for our growing strength, the influence of the devoted hearts she gathers, the steadfast power for good she has exerted.

John Wesley has become increasingly great and wonderful in my mind. There is a toughness—almost a ruthlessness—about him which would not have made service under his direction always a pleasure. He gave the orders and they were obeyed or a man walked no more with him. This, he insisted, was freedom and no man ought to complain. There is very little humor in him, and when he makes us laugh the most he would have been unaware that there was anything funny in the situation or in his reaction to it. What I am trying to say is that while Wesley believed in going on to perfection, a blind man could see his faults. But I admire his single-mindedness and have a

17

great desire to emulate it. His suspicion of the mystics strikes a responsive chord in my own suspicious mind. Wesley's combination of deep emotion and austere thought appeals to me. I like men with soft hearts and hard heads. The Methodist impatience with mushy do-gooders and its admiration for result-getters fits my temperament. Emerson and his son once tried to get a calf into the barn without success. Emerson pulled and his son pushed, but the calf refused to budge. Then the maid came along and, putting her fingers in the calf's mouth, easily led it inside. Emerson wrote in his *Journal* that night: "I like people who can do things." So do I.

The right to one's own opinion and the freedom of the pulpit are characteristic of the Wesleyan movement. Ours is a tradition of discipline and liberty. Methodist preachers will go where they are sent but they will also speak their minds. There was remarkably little foolishness in this eighteenth-century apostle of religion and common sense, and there was never any flabbiness. None of these qualities are unique but their combination gave us a unique person and a great heritage.

I have been set down among the brethren in places all over the world during these past years. Sometimes I have met men who thought their Methodism was merely a memory of something overshadowed by a united church or a new denomination. We have not talked together ten minutes before we had something in common and felt the bond of unity in a peculiar way. I have no doubt that this is true also of all religious fellowships, and it is a wonderful experience. This is the household of faith, or the particular spiritual family in which every churchman is at home.

An annual conference in our church is the basic organization. To such a conference every preacher belongs who is in full connection with the church. Men may be ordained who do not belong to a conference, and, in our polity, ordination is not more important than conference membership. I heard a man say that no labor union is as tightly ordered as a Methodist Annual Conference. There is something to it. Young men must fulfill the requirements of education, morality, and ability. Then they must be voted into membership. Their characters are examined and voted on every year and any flaw in their conduct makes them liable to expulsion. I know of no relationship more disciplined than membership in a Methodist Annual Conference.

A bishop of The Methodist Church has membership only in the Council of Bishops. Here is a group of rugged individualists as different from one another as men can be. No two of them run their offices the same way and no two of them but have large areas of disagreement. Yet I have not known on this earth a family as concerned for its members as is the Council of Bishops. These are my brothers and my fathers. When one of the greatest of them said to me on his retirement, "I love you like a son," the tears came into my eyes and my heart overflowed with joy. Who are my brethren indeed? These whose prayers sustain me and whose love upholds me.

A long time ago I came down the street with a friend and saw my father working in the yard of a building where he was the janitor. Because of a recurring illness he often had to do unskilled labor and take any job available. I was ashamed and steered my friend across the street and pretended I did not see my father. If he noticed—and I suspect he did—he gave no sign and never brought up the subject. My stupid snobbery never made any difference in our relationship, but it is the memory of my childhood that makes me most ashamed.

How many times have I done unworthy things which would have made the church question my worth to it! Yet, with an amazing tolerance and patience, it has held its peace and waited. It has shown the kindness and forgiveness of a parent and it has believed in me when I could hardly believe in myself. If I want to be critical of it, that is my business. If it needs to be challenged, we who love it will undertake the task. But let no outsider presume to either criticize or attack it.

I called the General Conference of The Methodist Church to order in Denver, Colorado, on April 27, 1960. We sang Charles Wesley's hymn for the opening of a conference: "And Are We Yet Alive?" The names of the bishops and delegates who had died were read. As we stood for a moment of silence, it came to me that I envied no one his background. Here were my people and this was my home.

19

□ □ □

WORDS   I do not know of any book in the world with such a majestic, wonderful opening sentence as: "In the beginning was the Word." The man who wrote it was inspired beyond all necessity for argument. When I was a student in the theological seminary, it was pointed out that there is much Greek philosophy back of the Fourth Gospel. I learned that John drew his picture of Jesus Christ against an ancient background. Some of the details need to be sharpened anew now and again from some books on my shelf. But the English sentence stands forth in sheer beauty and shines in its own light.

What wonderful things are words! For more than thirty years I have been using them professionally and striving to make myself a better craftsman. To endeavor so to speak that the words will march into the hearts of the hearers is the greatest thrill I know. To speak and watch the words bounce back like pebbles from a window is to experience despair and desperation. Or to write words down and strive to arrange them so they reveal the thought and emotion in the mind and heart is agony and triumph. A man once remarked to a writer that he supposed he liked to write. "No," was the reply, "writers do not like to write. They like to have written." What workman uses such exasperating and thrilling material? The uniqueness of man is established by his ability to speak and to write.

I cannot remember when I first began to read, though there is a hazy memory of a mighty moment when words and sentences first became clear and meaningful. My mother began to teach me before I started to school, for she had been a teacher. One day I read a sentence and then picked one out by myself. George Bernard Shaw said he could not remember a time when he could not read, and so assumed he had been born literate. That was not my case, but reading began so long ago for me that life without books is impossible for me to contemplate.

There was a great summer in my childhood which stands out as one of the times I came closest to unadulterated happiness. I was ten years old and we lived in Fresno, California. It was my last summer of leisure, for from then on I had some kind of vacation job on the farms about the valley. But this year my father gave me a summer membership in the Y.M.C.A. which allowed me to swim every morning. I rode my bicycle downtown each day and went swimming with about fifty other naked juniors. Then I went next door to the city library and returned the book taken the day before, browsed around for an hour, and went home with another book. I read that book the rest of the day and finished it before bed. Only Sunday interfered with this schedule—which did not make it a happier day in my immature judgment.

The stuff a boy will choose when he has no guidance! Some of it was junk, no doubt, and some of it was over my head. I read James Fenimore Cooper and Robert Louis Stevenson by sheer accident— their titles intrigued me. Some of the novels I chose gave me the impression that many adults were pretty silly and ridiculous. My mother was quite upset a few times when she saw what I was reading, but she never took a book away from me and she seemed to assume that common sense would carry the day and good writing would win the victory.

This is not to be recommended in a day when young people either do not read at all or else are fed a kind of mental baby food. When I hear all the discussion about what certain ages are ready to understand and what should be allowed at this or that stage of young life, I smile at my memories. I must confess that it is a satisfaction to have been born before there were so many child experts around. My own free and undisciplined ways led me into at least one experience which is curiously lacking in so many modern young people: I developed a love of reading.

Such an affection is a very precious possession. Some years ago it was my custom to ride the train across the continent three or four times a year. I read from early morning until late at night in a frenzy of forced draft stimulation. My fellow passengers were so often bored and listless. They looked out the window with blank faces, or went to the club car to breathe secondhand cigarette smoke thick enough to walk on. Or they chain-smoked as if they could hardly wait to welcome their lung cancer, and they drank. Or they gossiped with any captive listener in a continuous stream of platitudes and comment on the banal and trivial. And I thanked God that in his mercy he had led me into a love of books.

21

I have a strong sense of what ought to be read and what ought not to be read at certain times of the day. Even on a vacation I could not begin the day reading a novel. There is something immoral about it. In the morning, one reads theology or philosophy or history. Any man who would start off with a detective story should be watched seriously and trusted slowly. I admit he may still be a person of character, but he has given reason for suspicion. Let nothing frivolous be perused before noon.

Novels are all right after the day's work is ended and you have gone to bed. Then there is something quite proper about browsing through the fiction, especially if it has been a hard day, which most of them are. Detective stories are for Saturday night, and even then can be justified only if the week has been more difficult than usual. Magazines are for travel because you can tear out what you want and discard the rest. The luggage gets a little lighter thereby, which is always a pleasant experience. The trouble with paperbacks is that they resemble magazines and I treat them as such. I can even tear pages out of them and then throw them away, something I can never do with a real, hard-cover book.

I have a great suspicion of words that are capitalized—such as you find in the purple passages of lodge rituals or in the writings of the mystics. I never got much out of *Science and Health* because I never knew what the author meant when she talked about Light or Truth or Spirit. I know that these terms cannot be made too precise, but to throw them out without any explanation or definition that a pragmatically inclined mind can grasp is like trying to sell moonbeams in Woolworth's. The comment which was cherished most of all regarding my own feeble attempts to use words was given by the late Henry Sloane Coffin. He referred to a "lean and lucid style."

As a preacher, I find myself reading for a purpose, although it is a very broad one. I read to find material that will enable me to better preach the gospel. Nearly everything is grist for that mill, but it makes a man mighty impatient with abstractions and anything not closely connected with life. Everything has to mean something and it has to be capable of being shared with other men. Theology that cannot be preached is no good. Words, therefore, that are used simply as ends in themselves fail to arouse my enthusiasm because they fail to arouse any response.

I cannot help but say that the academic writers who have become the recognized spokesmen for the ecumenical movement—the National Council and the World Council—have done it more harm than all its reactionary critics put together. What ought to be a dramatic affair has turned into such dullness that the very word "ecumenical" makes a fellow sleepy.

There is a story about an author who needed money—a not unusual situation. He wired his publisher: "How much advance will you give for a novel of sixty thousand words?" The publisher wired back: "How big are the words?" Some of the stuff put out today seems to emphasize bulk and nothing else. How many books are written that would be much better if they were condensed! We develop jargon for every intellectual discipline so that two sentences will reveal what school the writer comes from and what high-sounding nonsense will be used to cover his lack of thought. Words are chosen with paralysis in their muscles and leukemia in their blood. Lifeless, dull, abstract, academic, they kill any interest a man might have in the subject. The mimeograph machine (that invention of the devil) enables every bore to spread his dullness across the earth and so mutilate and cheapen words that they become hated—or worse, unnoticed.

The mimeographed tripe that comes across my desk and slides rapidly into the wastebasket is simply terrifying. Every committee sends its minutes and every organization passes resolutions. Every secretary and every bureaucrat sitting around with nothing to do suddenly get the great idea: "Let's send out another mailing." I can only assume that everybody is a frustrated author and will get his dull words and tiresome style on paper if it kills him, and sometimes I wish it would. There is a law—call it Kennedy's law—that the less an organization is needed, the more printed matter it will distribute. And the corollary is that the less accomplished, the fancier will be the annual report.

But brethren, before you lose all control, turn back to the Bible. One of my former colleagues on a theological seminary faculty has pointed out that while the Greeks are the people of the eye, the Jews are the people of the ear. They have a sense of words and their language is alive. They speak, they tell, they announce, they proclaim. God has told them what is good and he has commanded them what to do. There in the Bible you will find speech that is living and vital and unforgettable and inescapable. The Old Testament tells the Joseph story in thirteen brief chapters, while Thomas Mann takes four volumes. Modern novelists write long books about biblical characters and make one tenth the impression made by the short verses in the Bible. Here is the book that knows about the miracle and wonder of words. "In the beginning was the Word."

Classrooms are the worst places so far as dead language is concerned. The educational experts develop a speech that is fit for no habitation save a cemetery. Any man who gets in a theoretical ivory tower is doomed ultimately to talk like a walking ghost. It is in the marketplace, the home, at the ball park, the shop, the church, where language is alive. Every man who would speak or write must be with all kinds of real people in all kinds of real situations. John Wesley and one of his preachers came upon two women quarreling near Billingsgate. Their language was forceful but not polite. The preacher suggested they move along, but Wesley said, "Stay, Sammy, stay, and learn to preach." Woe unto us when we withdraw to our closets and converse only with our own kind.

I listened to a long-winded speech on the floor of a conference not long ago. Turning to a friend of mine from Texas, I asked what the speech was all about. He answered: "A friend of his caught his tail in a crack, and he wants us to help him get it out." How pointed! How adequate! How fine!

It may be that one of this generation's greatest crimes is the debasing of our language. When I think of TV commercials, I get sick to my stomach. The Madison Avenue boys have done more to reveal the essential tawdriness of our civilization than any other single force. What shall our defense be when we stand to be judged by the One who said: "I tell you, on the day of judgment men will render account for every careless word they utter; for by your words you will be justified, and by your words you will be condemned" (Matt. 12:36-37).

I began preaching when I was eighteen and a sophomore in college. I have been proclaiming the good news ever since. How many sermons

24

have been preached in those years and how many words have been used? I wish my speaking had been better done, but it has been my best. Is there any other subject a man could talk about so much without exhausting himself and his hearers? None! For when we talk about the Word which became flesh, our own poor words become fresh, relevant, alive. The Word dwells among us, "full of grace and truth."

TEACHERS When I started to Hawthorne School in Fresno, California, in 1913, it never occurred to me that this was the beginning of a twenty-year sentence. I could not have stood it if I had known, for it looked rough enough to hold out until noon. When my mother left me to the howling monsters on the playground and the cold officials inside, it was one of those crises which the psychologists talk about. There may be an easier way to do it now; but for the bashful child, life is full of such agonizing experiences.

It is amazing how, after all these years, there are teachers who are remembered. Of course there were many who are forgotten, and why some are remembered and why "some there be that have no memorial" would be a worthy subject for research. It would probably reveal a great deal both about the teachers and about the students.

The first teacher I remember was Miss Snow White. That was her name, so help me, and one of the expressions of elementary grade humor which always put them in the aisle was to wonder what had happened to the Seven Dwarfs. Miss White was a blonde, as I recall, and very beautiful. In fact, I was so much in love with her that just to be near her was bliss. She lived at our home for a few days one time while waiting for her room to be redecorated, and that was heaven for me. I sat next to her at the breakfast table and again at the supper table in the evening. To start and close a day sitting next to Miss White was almost too much ecstasy for one small boy.

The next teacher I remember was Miss Hicks. She was not pretty like Miss White, and she was older. At least that is the way I remember her. She was austere and a strict disciplinarian. No one ever expected any break in the rather strict teacher-pupil relationship. But she was utterly fair, impartial, and objective. There was nothing mean about her, and I had a great respect for Miss Hicks. My memory is of competence and dignity. None of us ever got away with anything, but when we would sometimes refer to "old lady Hicks," there was no malice in it. I liked her and I never forgot her. It is not necessary to have everybody's liking, but it is necessary to possess integrity.

There was a teacher in an Oakland, California, school who never won my respect, and yet I remember her. She could not get things under control. Some of the older boys gave her a bad time, and I can remember that on more than one occasion she cried. This was embarrassing and it was all wrong. Yet she was amazingly kind to me on one occasion. I had written an essay that was very good, according to her. But a girl in the class pointed out bitterly that part of it was almost a complete steal from a recent best seller. She was correct; and although the material had not been taken consciously, I was guilty all right. But when I went to the teacher after class and tried to explain that I was not quite sure what had happened, she was so understanding that it made me cry. The incident had one very good effect in making me fear plagiarism and despise plagiarists.

Yet as the years have passed by, it has come to me that what seemed to be original ideas were only old ideas freshly adorned. Does a man ever have an original idea? The genius perhaps, but for most of us it is only giving our personal twists to questions and answers phrased long, long ago. But to take another man's form and style and repeat it like a parrot is so low-down it makes one ill. There was a very popular modern preacher whose well-meaning friends published his works after his death. It was discovered that some of it was taken word for word from other men, which is probably why he never published it while he was alive. But it was bad enough to preach it, and I could never share the rather general enthusiasm for the brother.

The principal of a grammar school was an awesome figure in my day. He came into the room now and again to see how things were going and he was always asked to make a few remarks. As I recall them, these little talks were no great shakes but full of moralisms with now and then a little feeble humor. We endured these visits but were glad when they were over. I was sent to the principal's office once for some unseemly behavior, and I was scared half to death. The old boy asked me if I was guilty, and I could not think of anything to say but Yes. This pleased him and he praised me for being so forthright and brave. I listened to a little talk on the nobility of confessing one's guilt and left feeling noble and brave. But it was all just a little bit phony, at least on my part.

English literature was always a favorite subject of mine but I had very few good teachers in the field. Most of them were mechanical in their approach, and studying poetry became about as inspiring as counting boards in a fence. I learned to hate Shakespeare along with most of my generation and to be properly suspicious of anything labeled "literature." We were indoctrinated into the philosophy that excellence was a synonym for dullness as we were assigned some of the Russian novelists and some of the classics like *Paradise Lost* and *Pilgrim's Progress*. On most of these subjects I changed my mind in later years, but it was a hard struggle. Many of my contemporaries never did change their minds, and so we have the discouraging spectacle of universal education creating universal mediocrity of taste and universal suspicion of "great" books.

But there was one high-school teacher who was an exception. He had a contagious enthusiasm and he read for us with interpretive skill. I learned reams of poetry and developed a real appreciation for both modern and classical authors. I remember that now and again he would daringly read a little from the Bible and make us see some of its beauty. I had read the Bible since I was ten years old, but usually with a view to gaining merit. This was quite a different matter. It was a great shock to learn some years later that this man had been dismissed from his profession because of a moral lapse. There is a penalty a man must pay for every gift, and the more talents, the more temptations. I wish there was some way to tell that man how at least one student remembers him with a great sense of obligation.

My chief interests have been more literary than scientific. One cannot live in the modern world, however, without being aware of how science shapes and directs our life. Yet reading in this field has been more of a discipline than a pleasure—which makes it all the more

27

remarkable that one of the teachers I remember best taught chemistry. It was my first view of the physical world with all of its mystery and miracle, and to me it was like Balboa seeing the Pacific Ocean or an astronomer discovering a new planet. Mr. Brown taught us and he was rough and tough. He took a special delight in refusing to listen to any excuses. He was a strict grader and I worked as hard for him as for any teacher in my life. He had the gift of illustrating general principles with specific instances, many of them from his own experience. I never knew what he had been before becoming a teacher, but evidently he had been around and had lived anything but a sheltered life.

My greatest teacher was Miss Margaret Painter, who taught public speaking and debate at Modesto High School in California. She found me floundering in the hopes and torments of teen-agedom and made the path straight. After being in her class a few weeks, I knew what I wanted to do. She had the quiet authority of quality and it was unthinkable to give anything less than the best in her class. I remember her saying after a public-speaking contest I won only because of the ineptness of my opponents, "That would have been good enough for some people." I think the highest praise she ever gave me was: "That sounds like you." She compared each person with his own potential and she took a very dim view of average performances from students who could do better.

There is no better preparation for an ambitious speaker than debating. It forces you to organize your material and to speak for a verdict. If I were to put down the greatest weakness in most of the speeches and sermons I hear or read, it would be lack of organization. No one is sure what the speaker wanted to say or what he was trying to accomplish. I have listened to speech after speech at conferences with no sharpness and no clear word. If only those poor souls had taken debating from Miss Margaret Painter! Then they would have made briefs and organized their material so that no one could doubt what they were saying or why they were saying it.

For two years I worked with her in debate and speech and there was never another teacher like her in my experience. My college instructors in public speaking were not worthy to tie her shoes. We gathered material in the library and we tried to foresee all the arguments of the other side. We learned to think on our feet and to probe the weakness of the other fellow's case. She taught me to speak without manuscript and to seek to persuade conversationally and not bombastically.

There were statewide public-speaking contests in which we prepared in a general field and then had an hour or two to prepare on a particular subject. There were oratorical contests in which twenty-minute orations were delivered. I thought I was on my own in all these endeavors, and that is a sign of great teaching and coaching. Looking back on it, I am more aware of the quiet guidance and help which were contributed without ostentation. My speaking, so far as style and approach are concerned, bear the marks of my high-school teacher, Miss Margaret Painter.

She was a great person. Without any preaching or moralizing, she affected the characters of all her students. Others may have had more glamour and sex appeal, but no one on the faculty was more loved. It has been many years since I last saw her, and to publicly express my debt to her makes me both proud and humble. I am proud of her and mighty humble that God gave me such a great teacher.

I think that education tends to be an abstract subject, but teaching is one of the most exciting professions. It is strange that when one considers his education, he thinks of teachers and teaching rather than of knowledge and facts. Not that the latter are unimportant of course, but only that we are persons and the ultimate truths for us are found in personal relations. And besides those we remember, there are the teachers whose presence influenced us and we knew it not.

Next to preaching, it seems to me that teaching is the greatest job. I find it hard to sympathize with the man or woman who leaves his profession because he can make more money in a factory. There are rewards which go far beyond monetary returns. But our time seems to say, "What is the good of happiness? You can't buy money with it." Teachers are dealing with the real issues and the relevant situations. How poor our civilization and life would be without them, and how barren would my life be without these memories.

THIS
DISTINGUISHED
AUDIENCE . . .

COLLEGE

COLLEGE   I was the first one in my family to go to college, though I cannot recall that there was ever any doubt about my going. It has not been until later years that some of the pride my father and mother manifested in having a son in college has made any sense. In my circle of high-school friends, everyone was going to college and it was nothing to make a fuss about. But it turned out to be more wonderful than I expected.

I started to the College of the Pacific in Stockton, California. It was a Methodist institution recently moved from San Jose, California, when I registered in the autumn of 1924. It was a small church school with less than a thousand students, and its campus was raw and new. Through some kind of accident I was elected president of the freshman class, and would have been off to four wonderful years if I had not been so poor. A friend of mine in the same financial straits joined up with me and we rented a room downtown, did our own cooking, and wondered from day to day how we could hold on till the end of the semester. Weekends found me in Modesto, thirty miles away, where I could eat at home and see my girl.

At the end of the first semester it was necessary to leave college and either go to work or attend the Modesto Junior College and live at home. I chose the latter, and after one semester I was appointed supply pastor of a little Methodist church in Riverbank, a small town ten miles northeast of Modesto. The church can stand anything, and when I think of those sophomoric sermons often borrowed in large measure from Charles R. Brown, dean of Yale Divinity School, I marvel at human endurance and at Christian forbearance.

Let me confess that when my friends were planning their weekends
—which included dances, parties, trips—I experienced an unholy envy.
So many things which sounded like fun were not considered proper
for a student minister. Besides, I must call on my members, check
on Sunday-school teachers, prepare a sermon. Yet this routine, beginning at eighteen, soon became such a part of my life that it was
like breathing. At least there were fewer illusions of the ministry
for me to get over when I left seminary. I was supposed to get one
hundred dollars per month, but it never worked out that way. There
was a heater to fix or a roof that leaked and my finances were always
precarious. But the people put up with me and were kind. I did
not realize it then, but actually they were the ones who should have
been paid.

The junior college movement is important today, especially in
California, and it provides extra education at comparatively low cost
for the student. It saved my life, and I can still remember teachers
who were outstanding. Two or three of them stimulated my mind
with what seemed like radical ideas and I recall being shocked that
there was more involved in the Civil War than a desire to free slaves.
But for the most part, this was a continuation of high school without
any marked contrast in the quality of the teaching.

There was an elderly maiden lady who taught literature with a
kind of sentimental moralizing that made me sick. But I guess I was
the only one who felt that way, for Miss Blank was supposed to be
a great teacher. We romped through world literature one semester
and listened to her hit the high spots with so much appreciation for
everybody that it was like watching syrup pouring over a waffle. I can
still hear her waxing eloquent over somebody's "philosophy of life."
Sometimes she was extremely coy and cute. But as I said, this is a
minority report and there are probably men and women my age who
remember Miss Blank as the inspiration of their lives.

We had a dean who had been an athlete and a coach. He was not
an eloquent man but he could speak directly and plainly. I remember
him putting a pin in a windbag on the faculty at a public meeting
one time, and although the fellow had it coming to him, I was embarrassed. The dean made a speech to my class and discussed college
traditions. We were one of the first classes in a new and traditionless

school, and most of us had come because of home conditions or because we could not afford to go to a real college. He said it was a great thing to inherit traditions and he knew that some of us were unhappy because Modesto Junior College was too new to have any. But, he went on, would we rather inherit traditions or create them? He pictured a school with a great future and we were the pioneers. I never forgot that speech, and I like to bring in the same point of view when dedicating a new church.

I was on the campus a few years ago and saw changes that made me gasp. Great new buildings, beautiful grounds, a large student body, and ivy on the walls—it looked like a real college with a long past. I am the world's worst alumnus and never participate in special reunions. This has been because of work and schedules which made my excuses legitimate, but I have no real desire for such meetings. To meet an old friend after many years is a pleasure, but organized nostalgia leaves me cold. Such gatherings impress me like D.A.R. assemblies and other ancestor-worshiping services. Page Dr. Freud!

I went back to the College of the Pacific after Modesto Junior College and graduated in 1929. This is not the best way to go to college, for four years is short enough in any case to get established and put down a few roots. But this has been characteristic of my life. I have at last spent a whole decade in the same city, which is a record. Considering everything, it is amazing that Pacific took me to its heart and gave me so many honors. Nothing has pleased me more than to have my picture put up with such notable alumni as Eddie LeBaron, who came much later and played football. An honorary degree bestowed years later is among my treasured possessions.

In my day the president was the late Tully C. Knoles. He was a great man and one of those leaders who commanded the respect of everyone. I cannot remember any student criticizing him or talking him down. It was simply accepted that he was above our right to treat him as an ordinary man. I do not mean that he was stuffy or lived in a tower, but only that his character was such that he commanded our admiration. He taught an orientation course to the freshmen in which he gave a survey of western civilization. It was an unforgettable experience. An institution may be more than the lengthened shadow of a man, but College of the Pacific was molded and shaped by the spirit of Dr. Knoles. And he made it great. I was always in awe of him and when, years later, we would meet and talk as friends, it was a high point in my life.

I was not much of a student and my college record shows only a *B* average as I recall. A fraternity elected me into membership though I could not afford to live in the house. Besides the demands of a church I served in Oakland, California, on weekends, I was married in my junior year. Such conditions do not give a fellow much time for fraternity life. My clearest memory is the initiation ceremony and being left far out in the country to walk home. I remember also being blindfolded and hearing some of the boys swearing until one unknown brother commanded, "Cut out the cussing. Kennedy is studying for the ministry." That made me feel pretty pious.

Dr. George Colliver was professor of Bible, and he was a great teacher. He opened up the world of the Old Testament in such a way that it remains for me the great book for the preacher. He taught a course in New Testament which brought Jesus to life more than all the Sunday-school lessons I ever had. He disturbed me, but in spite of violence done to my fundamentalist upbringing, my real love for the Bible was born in his classes. He was a social prophet himself and he believed in the practical application of his religion. There was a childlike quality about him which trusted everybody. I am still ashamed when I remember the term papers circulated through my fraternity and handed in year after year. Perhaps different readers made this deception possible, but Dr. Colliver would never have imagined anyone doing such an unethical thing. He flunked me in Old Testament, which makes me the only bishop in The Methodist Church to have failed a Bible course in college. Professor Colliver wrote me a note when I was elected to the episcopacy and reminded me that I still owed him a paper on Jeremiah.

The only extracurricular activity I participated in was debating. We met teams from England and Australia besides the American college and university debaters. The men from overseas were so informal and easy in their delivery that it made my high-school formality appear mechanical and immature. But I learned much from them and admired their ability to hang loose. I won fifty dollars one night by delivering a winning oration on temperance.

College was a terrific experience, and yet I am hard put to describe it convincingly. From the professors I got a critical attitude and a desire to see through the pretenses of human experience. There was a time when I must have been insufferable at home, for I remember trying patiently to set my father right on religion. The old man would stand it for as long as possible and then he would get mad. Enough was enough! We had to stay away from certain subjects if there was to be any peace between us. My mother could listen to radical ideas and smile without getting upset. She was always more adjustable and I think she was better educated than my father.

I was making an address at the College of the Pacific some time ago and a student speaker urged that the curriculum be made more difficult. I was shocked. In my day, we never asked for things to get harder but complained that we had so much to do. Of course when a fellow has to work his way through, he finds that studying takes all his spare time in any case. I keep wondering if just tampering with courses will produce citizens for our dangerous situation. As I remember, it was the rousing of curiosity, the developing of a respect for knowledge, the creating of a love for books and libraries that were the main things. Above all, it was confidence that the truth was worth seeking and following.

In a history class one day, an older student was waxing eloquent about the reactionary tendencies within the church. "Why," he said, "if Jesus Christ should return to earth today, not even the Salvation Army would take him in unless he could play a cornet." The professor smiled and pointed out some things about the church the student had overlooked. We felt good that we could think as we pleased and say what we thought. It was wonderful.

Students that have to be protected are not much count. Colleges that substitute prayer meetings for study halls are serving the devil. The arrogant narrowness which is called religion in some quarters never was encouraged on the Pacific campus. I left the college with faith in Christianity and confidence in the church. Some lumber had been thrown aside, but in its place there was assurance that God and truth were one. College was an experience so great that to think about it makes me want to thank God. There never was a greater creator of a greater tomorrow than the small church college.

□ □ □

SEMINARY   One late summer day in 1929, I climbed a hill in Berkeley, California, and registered at the Pacific School of Religion. It was one of those decisive acts which scared me a little, and I felt that a Rubicon had been crossed. Indeed, I walked around the block before getting the courage to commit myself to three years of theological study. It is hard for me to understand my feelings on that occasion, for a commitment to the ministry had been made long ago. But I felt like an arsonist burning bridges.

At a Quarterly Conference in the First Methodist Church of Modesto, in 1924, I received my local preacher's license, which is the first step in the Methodist ministry. I was a high-school junior, and there were five other boys who made the same decision and received their licenses that night. Dr. C. B. Sylvester was my pastor and his kindness and encouragement are among my happiest memories. I am the only one of those six boys who became a minister—most of them having gone into education. The only reason I can give for this happening is that I wanted like blazes to be a preacher. Yet entering seminary was a jolt.

My three years at the Pacific School of Religion were probably more significant than any other similar period in my life. I did not think so at the time, and this judgment comes from a larger perspective. If you meet great men when you are twenty, things happen to you that a thousand years will not change.

There have been some changes made in seminary education since my day, and I have been rather closely associated with some of them. It is a healthy sign that there is a continual ferment in all education, and it will be a sad day when the church assumes that its way of preparing men for its leadership is final. One of my friends, who had grown weary of a continual tampering with the machinery of the Annual Conference, told me one day that he supposed it was about time for the annual reorganization. I would rather go too far in that direction than stand still.

Yet I do not believe that anything of ultimate significance is being achieved through changing methods and techniques. Seminary to me was teachers, and the content of the courses was important ten to

38

one over methods. If a fellow has any common sense he will learn about administration and getting along with people. And if he has no common sense, there is no way to teach him these tricks anyway. But let a man who loves the prophets make them live for a student, and he has received something to stab consciences and create visions. Let a professor stand before his class as an exciting incarnation of Christianity and lives are changed forever. I will still prefer the log with Mark Hopkins on one end of it over the million-dollar plants with uninspired teaching.

To come face to face with serious scholars who assume that you are interested in being one also does something to one's ego. Professor William Bade in Old Testament was not the greatest teacher in the world, and there was nothing very dramatic about his presentations. But his quiet assumption that every student loved knowledge made a tremendous impression. Years later I was teaching homiletics at the school when Professor James Muilenberg was acting dean and professor of Old Testament. Sometimes, as I walked down the hall and passed his classroom, I would hear him talking about Amos with all the fervor of an old-time evangelist calling for mourners. That was a different kind of teaching from Dr. Bade's.

Professor George Hedley was young and filling in for Professor McCown, who was on leave. He was one of the three or four greatest teachers I have known. There was something awe-inspiring in the breadth of his knowledge, and he could talk as easily about music or art as about the New Testament. He followed me to Hartford later on and became a very dear friend. I never knew a man who made culture so attractive and desirable.

C. C. McCown was one of the outstanding New Testament scholars of his day. There was an austerity about him which made it most difficult to feel at ease with him. I wrote a thesis under his direction and had a conference every month or so. He liked the room cool and sometimes wore a kind of monk's robe to keep his blood from congealing. I remember him fondly whenever my secretary has to plug in an electric heater because the temperature of my office is too cold. I never left a conference with Professor McCown that it did not seem to me he must be saying to himself, "There is the most stupid student in the whole school."

Yet beneath his cool exterior there was a warm heart—which I only discovered some years later. He wrote a letter of recommendation for me in connection with a fellowship application which was so glowing it put me on a cloud for days. When I was asked to teach homiletics at the Pacific School of Religion some years later, he gave me a great thrill when, for the first time in a public meeting, he addressed me as "Professor Kennedy." In conversations with him about school matters, I found him to be not only a great scholar but a wonderful person.

The saint of the faculty was John Wright Buckham. He was kindliness, patience, concern, Christian love. His lectures in theology were sound but not very inspiring and, so far as I can remember, never controversial. In a liberal school, Dr. Buckham represented a more conservative voice from the past. I remember being critical and superior about him one time, which was then, is now, and ever will be the way of students. Another teacher shut me up completely with the quiet remark: "Well, whatever you want to say about John Wright Buckham's theology, just remember it has made him a good man. I hope yours will do the same for you."

There were other able men on the faculty whose courses made their contributions. But my own path led through their classrooms so quickly that they never stamped themselves as clearly on my memory as the ones I have mentioned. One of them was a pious-sounding fellow who was quite happy if you had his vocabulary memorized and used the words glibly as if they meant something. Another intrigued me for a time as a progressive thinker because he insisted that Paul led Christianity astray by making it too theological and too involved in Eastern mysticism. This progressiveness soon turned out to be shallow nonsense in my mind and I became a hero-worshiper of the apostle Paul, writing three theses on him and his thought. That professor influenced me in a negative way, and this is not to be regarded lightly. You may recall that George Bernard Shaw claimed a drunken father made him a teetotaler.

The spirit of the school was definitely liberal and free. As I look back on it, there was much overlooked or left out of its picture of the gospel. But this was the spirit of the time and it was necessary to break loose from a stultifying fundamentalism. It cured me of any hesitancy to listen to any man's ideas or to be afraid of any criticism of religion. It created in me a faith in plain speech and clear analysis. The shame which some of the brethren seem to feel unless Christianity is presented so that plain men are baffled by it never got into me. I think we often saw Christianity as too shallow and too humanistic in those days. But I rejoice that this was a part of my education and that this spirit affected the texture of my mind.

The student body was neither the best nor the worst. There were a half dozen first-rate minds and at least two whose brilliance impressed me. There was one class where I worked like a dog and received a *B*, because the professor gave only one *A*, and it was obvious that another student deserved it. Today that fellow is a professor whose knowledge of ancient languages forever amazes his colleagues. At least three others have done pretty well in their own fields.

There were a large number of fair students and a few stupid ones. The poorest dropped out of sight, and where they are or what happened to them, nobody seems to know. Some of the others I hear about from time to time, but there have been no close ties with any of my fellow seminary students. This was partly because we went into different denominations and scattered all over the country. Those who attend a denominational school have a tendency to form more lasting friendships, for there is always a group who go from school into the same Annual Conference. There are arguments for both kinds of seminaries and advantages to each. I have valued the interdenominational contacts of the Pacific School of Religion, but I would have learned more about Methodist polity earlier if I had attended a Methodist seminary.

There was not much social life during these years because there was no time for it. We had a few parties and meetings during the semester, but there was evening study involved and our weekends were filled. My wife was working as a secretary in San Francisco and we started early in the day. My student church was at Manteca, about seventy-five miles from Berkeley in the San Joaquin Valley. We drove to Modesto, fifteen miles further south, spent Saturday night with my wife's parents, and then spent Sunday at the church. There was Sunday-school responsibility, the morning worship service, and an evening preaching service. The Sunday afternoons were often taken up with pastoral responsibilities. We arrived back in Berkeley around 11 P.M. and were off again early Monday morning. It was hard work with no time off.

We had been following similar schedules ever since our marriage in college, and it never occurred to us that it was tough. Now it would seem unreasonable to ask many seminary students to follow such a routine, and the trend is in the direction of full time given to studies. There are obvious reasons for this and I am afraid that neither my church nor my studies received their due. But I learned from the beginning that the ministry is hard work and it became a habit early in my life. Perhaps this makes up for what might have been gained in the classroom. I still shudder when I remember closing weeks of the semester and the necessity of reading a book each night and being able to remember the main points for at least a day.

Two personal experiences stand out which came to me within the last three years. I talked with a boy in an eastern seminary who was serving a five-point circuit and trying to get a seminary education at the same time. He rode over country roads when the temperature remained below zero for days at a time. His wife was left alone with two small children for four days each week and he was gone most of the remaining three days. His superintendent told me that the people loved him and his churches were growing. His grades were average.

The other boy lived in a big city and was doing no outside work apart from his seminary program. His weekends were free for cultural interests and he listened to great preachers on Sunday. His grades were excellent, and he talked brilliantly about theology and philosophy. He was not sure whether he would be a preacher or teacher, but my guess is that he will end up on a faculty.

I do not know which boy will render the greater service to the church. I do not know which approach the church ought to encourage. Probably it is not a question of one or the other, but both. I wish the fellow with the circuit could have had a little more leisure for cultural affairs; and I wish the scholar had known some church experience that was less academic. One of the best suggestions came to me from a preacher who said a theological seminary ought to be not only a school but also a church. May the good Lord deliver us from the theological dilettantes, and may all theological learning be aimed toward the glory of God and the service of men.

DOCTOR   In the early part of 1931, I met the president of the Hartford Seminary Foundation and he told me about a fellowship I might apply for. It paid enough to help me through a year of study and there was a chance of renewal. There was one other feature connected with Hartford which intrigued me—they gave a Ph.D. degree. So when I was notified that the Jacobus Fellowship had been awarded to me, my wife and I made plans to enroll in that institution in the autumn of 1932. I wish it might be reported that this venture was launched with the purest of motives. But I went to Hartford because President Barstow had opened the door for financial aid; and I wanted a Ph.D. because I was tired of being called "Reverend."

Yet who can doubt that the Lord directs us to the place we ought to be! This was a marvelous three years in so many ways that it has always seemed that there was divine guidance. After more than a half century of living, the first article in my creed is that God directs the affairs of men and he guides every human life. I never felt that God tells me to order hamburger rather than pot roast on the merchant's lunch, as some of the Oxford Group brethren insist. But in the big issues, he gives us light enough for the next step.

We drove a 1929 Model A Ford across the continent and that was an unforgettable experience. It was loaded down with all our possessions, and my father-in-law prophesied breakdowns before we got out of California. But all that happened was a flat tire in Salt Lake City, and like the postal service, "not snow nor rain nor heat nor gloom of night" held us back from our appointed round. In those days, you could stay in cabins for one dollar a night if you had your own bedding. Seeing America first was not only thrilling but inexpensive.

We still remember Steamboat Springs in the Rockies. The aspens had turned yellow and gold, while the pines formed a dark-green background. Who can forget the tang of a Middle Western autumn? We stopped in Chicago and New York City. After we were settled in Hartford we spent weekends visiting New England towns. The man who has not driven over the Mohawk Trail in October does not yet know the full magic of this country. There is no need to travel abroad for the greatest scenery in the world; and if we can find a few more men to match our mountains, we will find our way through the present danger.

Since that time, I have traveled around the country a good deal and have been in every state. But that first transcontinental journey has a glory all its own. For we were young and on our way to a graduate school of theology. We were called to the greatest job in the world and we were discovering America. This was the pioneer movement in reverse, and the old looked new. Memory is man's ability to use time over and over again, and our "sentimental journey" is still a wonderful and continuing experience.

The Hartford Foundation consists of three schools: the Theological Seminary, the Kennedy School of Missions, and the School of Religious Education. My work was in the seminary, although a course or two was taken from professors of the other schools. It had a different atmosphere from the Pacific School of Religion, for it was more aware of continental theology and the European forms of Christianity. Barth was a familiar name and there were the first faint stirrings in the mulberry trees of what later came to be called neoorthodoxy. Indeed, one young New Testament professor preached a sermon in my student church on a special occasion which was so laden with paradox that not one single layman understood it. Barth might have followed his thought, but I am not even sure of that.

Once again the Lord gave some great teachers. There was Herbert Farmer from Cambridge, who later became John Oman's successor. He was more orthodox than some others I had known, and in some ways he was close to Bowne's personalism. He made clear to me by his own presence what Matthew meant when he wrote that Jesus spoke as "one having authority." There was the authentic ring in Farmer's teaching which carried deep conviction. I felt always that he was speaking out of an experience of God and at a level beyond argument. It was difficult to place him in the usual categories of liberalism or conservatism. His theology was at the same time profound and practical, and he was another man who put his stamp on my mind. I remember he taught by lecturing unless he was conducting a seminar, and his lectures kept me stirred up and excited.

He preached for me one night in my church in Collinsville, Connecticut. He arrived at the last minute, for the bus had "run out of petrol." One of my laymen spoke of the greatness of his spirit and the wisdom of his message. "Dr. Farmer knows more about God than any man I ever heard," was the way he put it. We called on Professor Farmer in Cambridge, England, a few years later and were received with such courtesy and hospitality that my wife and I felt like important people.

Another great professor was G. H. C. MacGregor, who later returned to Glasgow University. He was an outstanding pacifist and one of the most dedicated of all my teachers. He had written the Moffatt Commentary on the Gospel of John and his class in the Fourth Gospel was one of the high points of my education. He always opened his classes with prayer and was one of the few men who could pray with both dignity and intimacy.

MacGregor did not think much of the contemporary emphasis on religious education. At a banquet given in his honor before he left for Glasgow, he spoke with great frankness on this subject. He apparently felt that since he was leaving he would speak his mind once and for all. He referred to the nonsense of assuming that children know more about what is good for them than their parents or their teachers. I remember he commented that on the basis of this philosophy, Malcolm (his three-year-old son) would not drink his orange juice. It was great fun for me, who was not involved, but it left bitterness in the hearts of some students and faculty members.

Professor Alexander Purdy was in the New Testament department and he was chairman of my doctorate examining committee. He was a Quaker and invited his students to his home every Thursday night. My wife and I fell into the habit of attending these meetings where we sat in quietness for a half hour with a dozen or so other students. At first this was not easy for noisy Methodists, but we came to find refreshment in the quiet worship experiences around a fireplace. Dr. Purdy had the calm integrity characteristic of Quakerism at its best.

There were three retired men whose influence had been great in the school. Former President MacKenzie appeared on special occasions and he was much respected and loved. Professor Jacobus invited me for lunch one day since I was the recipient of the fellowship named in his honor. He sent his car and chauffeur, which impressed me greatly, and he was the soul of courtesy. Former dean Rockwell Harmon Potter was retired but his interest in the students lived on and he was kind to me on several occasions. Years later, when I was giving the Beecher Lectures at Yale, there was a series of loud "Amens" from one corner of the chapel. I thought it must be some old Methodist brother, but it turned out to be Dean Potter showing his approval and support of a former student.

My aim for several years had been the attainment of a Ph.D. It seemed to me that having accomplished this one thing, my life could be called a success. This was a strange thing and I suppose it reflected an intellectual hunger and an academic pride—probably more of the latter. At any rate, it made me single-minded and it taught me that happiness is primarily moving toward a desired goal with all your might. Those were great days.

Languages were neither easy nor enjoyable as a rule, and I struggled with them valiantly. Greek, however, was more of a pleasure than I expected, and it came with surprising ease. I started German on my own and took a course at Hartford. The long—and, to my English mind, involved—syntax of the German theological writers did not make that subject my favorite. You remember the two students at a dull theological lecture in German. One said, "Let's go." But the other replied, "Let's at least wait for the verb." French had been taken in college and reading it was a pleasure. Like most of my kind, I dropped the languages as soon as the examinations were passed, and today I read the New Testament in English.

My thesis was on the subject *Human Nature According to St. Paul*. It was pretty dull, but the main theme has undergirded my theology and my preaching. Paul, I found, had no confidence in human nature apart from God. But he was not the pessimist pictured by some

46

theologians, for the natural man was not so much depraved as powerless. The spiritual man has discovered the resources of God, and he is saved because he knows his own weakness and God's adequacy in Christ. It took longer than this to say it, but that was the main idea.

One of the best things about the whole business was that I read the Letters of Paul not once but many times. That a man could write about the problems of the churches, the quarrels of members, the doctrinal squabbles, and produce great devotional and theological literature is a miracle. Here was a man who comes along not more than once in a thousand years. Just to be with such a person and to learn something of his mind was simply overwhelming. The degree was only secondary in importance, though I learned this much later.

On a beautiful day in May, 1934, I became the Rev. Dr. Gerald Kennedy. My wife and a few friends acted as if it were quite an event, and the people of my church expressed congratulations and seemed properly impressed. But the glory soon faded and quicker than seemed possible, it was practically forgotten. If the degree was ever worth a dollar to me in salary, I never discovered it. I still had to work on my sermons and it provided no oil for the machinery of personal relations. But it was something completed and its by-products were precious and lasting. Perhaps the most important results of the whole affair were the discipline involved and an understanding that once you have started something, you must stay with it to the finish.

Now and again a young preacher thinks that if he can go back to school and get an advanced degree, he can move ahead. Hardly ever is this true. The ministry is not dependent on academic degrees, and usually when a man's service is sick, another degree will not heal it. In one of my conferences the hardest man to appoint to any church had a Ph.D. The main thing is to develop the habits of study and go down deep when it comes to the great themes of the Christian faith. Nevertheless, I still believe there are much worse obsessions than the attainment of a doctor's degree.

It is a good thing when the ministry can meet the learned professions on their own ground. Certainly earned degrees are of some value in winning a hearing at the university. But the seminary giving the impression that to be a professor is a higher calling than to be a pastor should not be tolerated by the church. Nor should students be encouraged to spend too many years taking a few more courses and getting one more degree. I have seen young men appointed to churches after this experience whose preaching ability was ruined. They tried to make the congregation a seminar of graduate students and they emptied the sanctuary so fast that you would have thought it had been declared off limits.

A PRIVILEGE
TO BE HERE...

EUROPE   My student church in Connecticut was the First Congregational Church of Collinsville, a small village about fifteen miles west of Hartford. There was a time when it seemed that New England Congregationalism was just what the doctor ordered. I liked the intellectual climate; and the lack of pressure was as pleasant as dropping into an easy chair after a hard day's work.

This fine church called me to its pulpit shortly after arriving in Hartford. For I had soon grown weary of having free Sundays. Seeing little chance of employment through the regular seminary channels, I went out on my own and caught the Collinsville church in a weak moment. They were divided between two candidates and wide open for a compromise choice. I was called on one Sunday, bought five rooms of furniture on Monday, and moved into the parsonage on Friday. It was good to be preaching regularly again. Bishop Francis Asbury, who had to stay in hiding during the Revolutionary War, complained of "the dumb and silent Sabbaths." After a few Sundays without preaching, I decided that finances had nothing to do with it. Sundays were made for preaching.

What a wonderful welcome was given us by those New Englanders. There was no personal responsibility for finances, little was expected beyond a sermon on Sunday morning, a few meetings with the Sunday-school teachers, a few calls, and a monthly meeting of the Standing Committee. I had never had it so good. In addition, they raised my salary when my doctorate was obtained.

But Methodism was in my blood and I began to miss the organization, the quotas, the pressures, the programs. The tranquil life of the village bored me, and my inability to make the church grow

51

troubled me. Without the tension of seminary I began to disintegrate, and it was all the more disturbing because there was no apparent reason for it. Study became difficult and the days were long. I dreaded going to bed at night knowing how bleak the morning would appear.

I was saved by a trip to Europe which we had been planning for a long period. My wife and I had a close friend who was a premedical student at Columbia University. He was financially in good shape and we began to plan a bicycle trip through Europe. I had written a term paper for him on the subject: "Medicine From Hippocrates to Galen" in exchange for a weekend in New York. He received an *A* for it and was saved from a real possibility of failing the course. The ethics involved never entered my mind at the time, and it gave me a friend who has been very close to me for many years.

As certain complications arose, it seemed wiser for my wife to go back to California with her family while I made the trip. This was not the first, nor was it the last time, that she gave up something she wanted to do for me. For my part, there was many a day when I would have given up the whole experience to see her, and the four months were among the longest I have lived.

Those were the days when it was much more unusual to travel abroad, and for me to see Europe seemed like a miracle. This was something for the rich, and that anybody so poor could actually have such an experience was wonderful indeed. I wish I could describe all that went through my mind. Since that time we have traveled a good deal, and being in a foreign country has become commonplace. But that first sight of the European coast was as exciting as seeing a new planet.

We went by freighter from New York to Le Havre. There were eight passengers altogether and the others were good fellows and enjoyable companions. We ate with the officers, had the run of the whole ship, shaved when we felt like it, and had ten days of complete relaxation. There is nothing to compare with a sea voyage for rest, recreation, and restoration. We sighted an old sailing ship in the grain race from Australia to England, just before sighting land, and it seemed the proper introduction to the Old World. As I recall, the passage cost sixty dollars.

My first experience in Le Havre threw me into a panic because my suitcase was left on the back of a French taxi. But an Italian professor who spoke French helped us run down the taxi and soon we were off on the boat train to Paris. We were guided by another professor and fellow passenger to a little hotel on the Left Bank where we found a room on the third floor that was both clean and cheap. It was not far from the Boulevard St. Germain. Twenty-three years later I was in Paris and spent a morning wandering through that same neighborhood and found the old hotel just about the same. It had a different proprietor but the smells in the halls had not changed.

Paris so captured us that we could hardly bring ourselves to leave. We wandered along the Seine, sat in the Tuileries, walked up the Champs Élysées, explored Montmartre, and drank coffee at sidewalk cafes. Our favorite restaurant was the Café Procope where Diderot had spent many an evening. For sheer style and elegance, I do not know another city in its class. It has a kind of worldly luxury and charm about it that seems to speak of assured position and pride. Chesterton once remarked that if they would give him the luxuries, they could keep the necessities. He could have been thinking of Paris. We bought bicycles which were English-made and altogether satisfactory. They cost about fifteen dollars in our money and I sold mine a little more than three months later for ten dollars, so that transportation was not much of an expense. One morning, with our clothes in knapsacks strapped on the back, we headed north. We went on through St. Quentin and into Belgium. I remember that prices were so reasonable that we liked Belgium immediately. Brussels, Ghent, Brugge, Ostende showed us their treasures and in nearly every place we met interesting people.

One thing impressed me then and the impression has been strengthened with the passing years. Foreigners in Europe bring out the best in the people. They enjoy trying to talk to you and they seem to consider it a privilege to help you with directions. I have been almost embarrassed by the way people have put themselves out for me. In spite of a growing anti-American feeling in some parts of the world, I have been treated rudely not more than twice, and that was in England after the Suez crisis. Americans so often look down on people who speak with an accent or are obviously strangers. We are a warmhearted people, but we are not always a polite people. The attempt to make 1960 a big travel year for the United States did not succeed as well as had been hoped. One main reason was the discourtesy which sometimes begins with the customs inspector and is continued by the cop on the corner and the passerby in a hurry. We ought to be courteous because we are human, but in our day, we had better learn courtesy as a weapon in the cold war, if for no higher purpose.

I had a wonderful time in Ostende because of the friendship of a professor from New York University who introduced us to one of his friends from an old Belgian family. Later on, I came back by myself and traveled the country with this man who knew its history, its culture, its traditions. The days spent in his company were an education. Yet I never saw him again and although our friendship was priceless to me it was a passing experience. He was one of the most interesting men I ever met and also one of the best.

We made our way through Holland, where the clean, neat country and scrubbed cities made us feel that we were in a well-kept parlor. The food was excellent and I was always hungry. I went to bed every night wishing it were time to get up and eat breakfast. We often rode one hundred miles in a day through sunshine and rain. Everything tasted good, partly because I was hungry, but I think the bread alone made the meals fit for a king. Why we serve the washed-out, tasteless stuff we call bread when Europe gives you delicious ryes and wheat delights, is more than I know. I cannot comprehend why we take out all the vitamins and taste only to put the vitamins back in again. Too bad we cannot learn how to either put the taste back too, or else to treat the flour with respect in the first place.

We were in Germany during the rise of Hitler. We awakened many a morning to the sound of marching, singing youth on their way to work in the fields and on the road. Soldiers were everywhere. In Hamburg we met a family with one son and a nephew who were outspoken in their opposition to the Nazis. I never heard from them again, and I have often wondered how many felt as they did. Most people I met either kept silent or spoke of all that Hitler had done for the economy. Looking back, it is easy for me to see how blind people can be to the real issues, and I doubt that any nation has a monopoly on that blindness.

There were unforgettable views in Germany and Switzerland. I rode up the Moselle Valley to Trier all by myself and watched the farmers working on the terraced vineyards. In 1960, my wife and I followed the same route in a car and I relived the experiences of twenty-five years ago. I am glad that I first saw the Alps and the Swiss cities on a bicycle. The sound of the cowbells awakening me in an Alpine village is a clear memory, and years later I brought one such bell home with me. All of this has been repeated several times in the last years, but I find myself comparing everything with the first time I was there.

I am glad I saw Berlin before the war. In 1950, I went with the Sherwood Eddy Seminar to Europe and we flew into Berlin. From the air it looked like the excavated ruins of some ancient biblical city. The bombed-out buildings, the broken statues, the piled-up rubble, and the people living in caves spelled the end of a wonderful city. Yet in 1959, West Berlin was rebuilt and prospering. First we tore it down and then we helped build it up. But the industry and the courage of the German people are great qualities and there was no sitting around waiting for someone else to start the work. Cities are, after all, people, and not primarily buildings.

My friend and I parted the latter part of July. He was tired and one hundred miles a day was too much. For nearly six weeks I was by myself and at times it was a lonely business. Language was uncertain and it seemed a long time since I had seen my wife. It was better to keep moving; and after Switzerland, I rode to Paris and then back to Ostende. My Belgian friend knew the driver of a sight-seeing bus who invited us along whenever he had two spare seats. We went to Holland, to France, to Canterbury. It was a fine conclusion to a full summer.

The return voyage took sixteen days because of heavy storms. To make it worse, we came into New York harbor on Sunday and could not get off the ship until the next day. Then it was across the continent by bus to spend a few days with my wife's family, always favorites of mine and a second family to me. (I have never been able to appreciate mother-in-law jokes.) Then back to the church in Connecticut. I have always felt guilty in leaving Collinsville three months after my four months' leave. But my bishop wanted me to return and there was an opening in January of 1936, so I returned to California. The people of the Collinsville church were wonderful and showed no resentment, although they must have felt that I owed them a longer pastorate.

The most amazing part of this whole experience was the new view it gave me of my own country. No man knows his native land until he has wandered in other countries, just as one needs to study other languages to appreciate his own. I saw the size of America and the great spaces. The freedom and the opportunity for all men were now more than speeches on the Fourth of July. In the talks I made, I spoke as much about my rediscovery of America as I did about my introduction to Europe. I am glad that more of us are traveling every year. It is good, of course, to see other places and peoples so that we can have a more sympathetic and understanding viewpoint. But it is even better to see ourselves in the big perspective and learn what the issues are. I came to see that travel is one of the best investments a man makes, for it will warm his heart with memories just as long as he lives.

I think, also, that a pilgrimage teaches a fellow a lot about himself. He learns something about his personal resources—or lack of them —and this self-knowledge is a necessity in growing up. Loneliness is a great teacher.

CALVARY   My first church after leaving seminary in Connecticut was the Calvary Methodist Church of San Jose, California. I remember complaining to a ministerial friend about how tough that church was, and he said, "Brace up. You are not the only man whose appointment leads to Calvary." I recognized it was true, but I was not much cheered. The first year after seminary was the unhappiest of my life, and only the grace of God and my wife kept me from going off the deep end.

I do not know if other professions demand the same difficult adjustments after professional training. I do not even know if all preachers go through what I experienced. But to me, moving from seminary to my first full-time pastorate was something that shook me up and almost shook me apart. This was strange, in a way, for I had served student churches from the time of my sophomore year in college. One should have been prepared, but there were marked differences. I shudder to think what would have happened to me if the modern system of limiting the amount of outside work a seminary student can carry had been in force. I could not have endured any greater adjustment.

For one thing, a preacher has no time clock. Suddenly there is no eight o'clock class and no term paper or book report due. The majority of men think this is exactly what they want most, but to be thrown into a situation where you must set your own schedule, provide your own discipline, choose your own order is not heaven; it is weariness and pain. You wonder if you are putting first things first and a nagging conscience whispers that you could have put in more time and expended more energy.

There is no measurement of what one has accomplished. Are you getting anywhere or is anything being done? Who can know? People, for the most part, are kind and appreciative though the critics are never entirely absent. Maybe it is better than it was last year, but you were not here last year and it is not very good today. I helped my wife's uncle build a garage one summer vacation and enjoyed it because at the end of the day, I could see what we had done. So many nails had been driven and so many boards were now fastened to the framework. I tell you, it was wonderful. But for the young preacher there is only a constant struggle to gain an inch here and prevent a backwash there. Sometimes it seems that the best he can do is try to hold the line.

Then there is the loneliness. Gone is the stimulation of the professors and the students. You are as isolated as the Ancient Mariner and the days stretch endlessly ahead. Sometimes you feel that not even God knows where you are—you are positive the bishop has forgotten. Suddenly, or so it seems, you are thrown out into an indifferent environment where no one knows and no one cares whether you survive or die. I found myself longing for any job that would give me orders.

Not the least of the problems was the indifference of many of the members of the church. Their attitude seemed to be, "Well, let us see what you can do. We do not expect very much and we shall be surprised if you make it." There were some wonderful exceptions who gave of their time and their money in a complete dedication of themselves to their church. But the bulk of the membership were about as devoted to Calvary Methodist Church as San Francisco is to Los Angeles. When you have only a few more than one hundred members, this makes quite an impression on a young preacher. Part of this spirit was due to a heavy debt, an unfinished building, a leaky roof, and a previous scandal.

Looking back on it, I think a great deal of my despair was brought about by the spirit of the age. The thirties were not a period of religious awakening or spiritual enthusiasm. People did not go to church in large numbers and many bright fellows felt they had outgrown such nonsense. The contrast with the present mood has been forgotten, but I can recall the poor, watered-down faith which most of us felt was all that science and truth had left us. The tide was flowing the other way and in spite of the fact that they were getting mighty good sermons at Calvary, the best I could hope for was a church "comfortably filled"—which is to say there was always room for everybody to have three feet between him and anybody else.

I went through a crisis which was like a second conversion to me. I knew I could not continue as I was and if God did not do for me something which I could not do for myself, it was curtains for my chosen vocation. Then it came to me that if God had called me to the ministry, he had some responsibility for me and my work. He would see to it that people came to hear me preach and he would take my poor but honest efforts and use them for his purposes. If he wanted me to do the job, then he must be willing to give me the power to do it. All of this and more poured out of my soul in prayer.

I cannot say that the end of all doubt came with this experience, nor is it true that all my living became sheer joy. But the main thing had been accomplished and it was never the same again. A friend of mine who was not a churchman once put it in a rather striking way. He said it was like having to pass a bully on the corner or else run away to the other side of the street or go around the block. You have a friend who says that he knows you can take care of the fellow if he makes trouble, but if you cannot, he will help you. This would not please the theologians, but it was the heart of my new experience.

John D. Crummey was a great layman in San Jose who took us into his home until we found a house. He was a member of the First Methodist Church but he lived in my parish. More times than I can remember, he encouraged me to believe that Calvary Methodist Church had a future and we were making progress. Sometimes on a Sunday night I would confess my doubts and raise the problems and he would give me new courage. Such men are the salvation of the ministry. Paul Davies, one of America's brilliant industrial leaders, joined my church to give leadership in the financial program. There was mighty little to lead and I have since wondered how it must have seemed to a man who dealt with millions to discuss an annual budget of not more than three thousand dollars.

There was a group of young married couples who took us in and were loyal to the church and to my ministry. Their friendship became so important to us that we probably made it too exclusive a thing for the good of the church. We met together every Saturday night for dinner and bridge, which was not the best preparation for Sunday morning, as I have learned since that first pastorate. There were other wonderful friends and members whose remembrance lifts up my heart. I learned something in that first church which has proved true in every church I served. Always there have been better saints in the pews than in the pulpit. Now and again there is a mean man or woman who wants to rule or ruin. We find from time to time, unfortunately, some small, frustrated, bitter person who thinks the church is the place for him to vent his meanness. But these are few and far between. Methodist laymen are the most wonderful people in the world. They put up with a lot and they are patient with bungling. They maintain a free pulpit even when they disagree with much that is being said in the pulpit. Nearly everybody wants to like the pastor if he will give them a chance. Most of them will respect even a difference of opinion, if they believe in the preacher's integrity and sincerity.

We had a fine Woman's Society of Christian Service. They were never content with second-rate productions, and whether it was a dinner or a worship service, it was done well. One of my young preachers told me one time that the gospel ought to go first class. He did not mean that it ought to have special privilege, but that it should be ashamed of anything but first-rate productions. I agree, and those women taught me that the church's standards must be second to none when it comes to meetings or programs. On one of those Christmases when we were broke as usual, the Woman's Society gave us a check for one hundred dollars. The note said we might find it useful. What an understatement! It saved our life.

I learned something about pastoral calling in that first parish, which was that I did not like to do it. One of the hardest things of my ministry has been making calls on people, and I do not know why it is. But to ring a doorbell has taken more courage at times than proposing to my wife. My district superintendent suspected this reaction and he would check on me regularly. When I met him he would say, "How many calls did you make yesterday?" I would try to explain that yesterday was a special situation but he showed no sign of being convinced. Since I never knew when we would meet and since his question was always the same, I fell into the habit of making enough calls today so that if I saw him tomorrow, he would be satisfied.

And with the passing years, I am more convinced than ever of the importance of pastoral work. A young preacher told me he had a psychological block when it came to calling. I said to him, "Son, I have had it all my life. So what?" It is a good thing to learn that some things have to be done whether you like to do them or not. A friend of mine who drifted from the church and came back wrote to me about how wonderful it was to have the pastor call in his home. I was having a routine checkup in a hospital one time and a young preacher came in and had prayer with me. It was one of the unforgettable experiences of my life. Some men enjoy this work, and they are fortunate. But whether a man enjoys it or not, it will be one of the main contributions of his ministry. For, in our time, to know that one man is interested in you as a person is like finding a cool spring in the desert. And, not least, pastoral visitation keeps the preacher aware of real people and real situations.

San Jose took me in and allowed me to become a part of the city's life. Those were the days when there was something wrong if every night was not filled with a meeting or a speech or both. The preacher represents his church and, like it or not, a large part of his work is public relations. There was no pay connected with these efforts, for the world usually gives men monetary rewards when they need them the least. But as I began to feel at home, my ministry became a joy and satisfaction. It may be that community activities were overdone, but they helped to make the city aware that there was a small Methodist church out in the suburbs.

One of the most pleasant experiences in those days was my relationship with the ministerial association. Such an organization, existing in nearly every community, is made up of the Protestant ministers and sometimes includes the Jewish rabbi. It was a high moment for me when I became president of that group, for they were fine friends and loyal colleagues. Believe me, we have differing church institutions, but we do have a world church in terms of fellowship and unity of the spirit. The Congregational minister was a father confessor to me and as often as not, men of other denominations were my closest friends. There were theological differences, but if there was anything but mutual respect and affection, I never knew it.

Remembering one's first church is bound to be inaccurate. The past is always shrouded in clouds and we have a way of censoring all our experiences even when we try our best to be honest. But concerning the debt I owe to that congregation, there is no doubt. I hope that every young preacher may be as fortunate as I was in the first people to whom he may be appointed or called. Out of what seemed to be the worst experience came the best. When, after four years, I was appointed to another church, I left with a deep sense of loss. I had arrived at one clear conviction which has never left me. I knew I was called to be a minister of Jesus Christ in The Methodist Church, and it was the greatest calling in the world.

□ □ □

PALO ALTO   My appointment to the First Methodist Church
of Palo Alto was made in June, 1940. Although only about sixteen
miles from San Jose, it was an entirely different community, the
main reason being Stanford University. This great educational institution profoundly influenced the life of the small city, much more
than San Jose State College was able to dominate its larger community. Besides, there was little home industry and many men
worked in San Francisco, making Palo Alto a bedroom suburb. There
was an intense pride in the town and a pronounced, and sometimes
self-conscious, sense of intellectual quality.

I never lived in a finer place. There was good music, a civic theater,
lectures, a nearly perfect climate, and ideal location. It was the kind
of place one would like to find after years of wandering, but it came
to me at the beginning of my ministry. This has happened to me
several times. I was elected a bishop at forty years of age, which is
regarded as young for that office, and four years later I was appointed
to the Los Angeles Area. This seems to me the most wonderful part
of the church, and one of my colleagues commented that the latter
years of my life would be anticlimax. I am not worrying about it,
but there were some of my ministerial brethren who thought a fellow
ought to go to Palo Alto only as a reward for many faithful years of
service.

This was not because the Palo Alto Methodist Church was so big
or so rich, but because it represented culture and status. I found, however, that churches do not vary as much as many people assume. A
few more professors, perhaps, and a few more college graduates in
the congregation, but nothing really different. One of the biggest
mistakes preachers make is to assume that they have to tailor their
messages to special groups. There are men who fall flat on their faces
because they try to get intellectual in one pulpit and folksy in another.
The intellectuals are bored with such sermons and the plain people
are outraged. The gospel is universal and while some illustrations may
pack more punch in some situations than in others, the essential
message is the same for all.

But Palo Alto was a testing place. The Stanford Chapel had the great preachers of America in its pulpit Sunday after Sunday. Dr. Elton Trueblood was the chaplain, and he either preached himself or had guests whose names were known nationally. I went into my pulpit every Sunday morning knowing that anyone in the city could hear a much better sermon at another place. It made me work to the limit of my ability and to preach the very best I knew how. Of course, I had been doing that already, but there was something about Palo Alto which seemed to imply that exhaustion was not enough.

Yet this was a most stimulating environment. It does help a man to be around scholars and to live where the intellectual affairs are taken seriously. It makes a man extra careful with his historical and literary references, and that is good. You can hardly talk carelessly about any subject if a man who teaches that subject is listening. Every now and then some member of the congregation would check an exaggeration or challenge an assumption, although it was always done with kindness and love. They were large-minded people, for the most part, and my short pastorate there was full of personal satisfaction.

I began a schedule that, with some small modifications, I have held to ever since. Arising at 5:30 A.M., I was in my office a little after six. Those early hours have become my power plant and they mean more to me than double their amount later in the day. Being a spiritual son of John Wesley, it was laid upon me that time is precious, no one should waste time, and the best thing was to arise early. It seemed to me at one time that Wesley overdid this emphasis on time. But the passing years have brought me around more and more to his point of view. One of man's chief sins is using time unprofitably or wasting it in meaningless activities. Let a man have two to three hours to himself at the beginning of the day, whatever his work or his purpose, and he will discover a new source of power.

In those years I met a young attorney on his way to his office at about the same time each morning. We would stop a moment and greet each other and became friends, although we never spent any time together socially. He belonged to another church but we met at a service club and this was the extent of our friendship. Yet I felt very close to him and I think he felt the same way about me. For he wanted to be the greatest lawyer in the country and I wanted to be the greatest preacher in the world. We were united only in our common determination to be the best we could be in our chosen professions.

It has come to me since then that the bond that unites people is a common purpose, which is serious and significant. Men do not create fellowship out of carousing together or seeking amusement together. They do not even find it by spending time together at social functions. They find it when they have a common attitude toward work and life. When the going is tough and the attacks are fierce, then the men who are united with you in maintaining a brave witness and an honest confession are strength and inspiration. To stand shoulder to shoulder with another man in fighting for a difficult but noble purpose is the real fellowship.

This was the period of the beginning of World War II. I can remember sitting at the radio with my brother-in-law and his wife listening to the careful, calm English voice of Britain's king announcing that his country was at war with Germany. That happened on September 3, 1939, over the Labor Day weekend, while I was still in San Jose. One tries to imagine what this means, but I doubt if any person could have known all that was involved in that terrifying announcement. Then followed the "phony war," when all seemed to be quiet in Europe. We learned later that this was simply the lull before the terror soon to be unleashed by the Nazis.

It was a time of serious soul-searching and inner turmoil. What did I believe about pacifism and the Christian response to war? It had been clear enough in my student days, for then war was only a racket promoted by munition makers seeking a profit out of death. But the Nazis were something different. The Jews were more than profits; they were people. When, in the spring of 1940, Germany began her next campaign and rolled relentlessly across Europe, neutrality and pacifism became more difficult to proclaim with conviction. If only the Nazis were losing, the problem would be solved. But they were not, and it was becoming daily more apparent what the world would be under their rule. When France fell on June 22, 1940, and the remnants of Britain's army managed to get back across the Channel without its armor or supplies, everybody expected the British to sue for peace. But they did not. In the words of a recruiting poster of that day, they said, "Very well, then. Alone."

I came to the conclusion that I was incapable of standing aside without resisting by force if force were available. Since that time, doctrinaire positions have had no appeal to me. There are great principles by which a man must live, but there is no way to be sure what those principles may demand in certain situations. I abhor the doctrinaires of both the right and the left. The fellow who accepts a certain logic and then follows it as far as it will go ends up in an impossible dilemma or in an insane asylum. Life is not like that, and whether we are talking about economics, or politics, or theology, we had better believe that life is bigger than our logic. This, I take it, is existentialism, at least one brand of it. There is the moment, the decision, the man, and God. None of us are smart enough to work those elements into a blueprint that will be exactly right when the situation is upon us.

On December 7, 1941, Japan attacked Pearl Harbor. Again the news came by way of the radio and we knew that our time of indecision was over. This was it and we were in it. We learned of the catastrophe and some reports indicated that we were defeated before we began. Invasion of the Hawaiian Islands was expected at most any time and the whole West Coast was alerted. We had our first blackouts; and walking around the block one night I discovered how dark a city is when there are no street lights and no moon. The young men were leaving and everything was an emergency.

I can still remember the miraculous sense of unity that developed almost overnight. From a divided, uncertain people we became a nation with one purpose. I contrast that spirit with the time we are living in just now and it brings me small comfort. For today we are divided by extremists from the left and from the right, with both sides doing their best to sow dissension in government, schools, churches. Does it take a war to unite the people? Will we ever be able to show the same sacrifice and the same single-mindedness for the constructive work for peace? Apparently, as Chancellor Adenauer one time put it, God has made man with limited intelligence but with no limit set for his stupidity.

Palo Alto is a level town and some of us began to ride bicycles to save gasoline and tires. I made my calls on a bicycle and enjoyed it while feeling better than ever before. Not long ago a friend told me that Dr. Paul Dudley White, the famous heart specialist, had said to him that people ought to ride bicycles to keep fit. Our civilization seems bent on robbing us of needed exercise in the name of progress. We no longer shift the gears of our cars or even wind our watches. Our great national sickness is overweight, but such things as walking, riding bicycles, or doing some physical work around our homes are too simple. We must join a gym and use fancy machines to control our weight.

My church was committed to a free pulpit, and while there was an occasional disagreement with my interpretation of the Word in wartime, there was never a crisis of any kind. Some of my ministerial friends had difficult times in maintaining their pacifist witness and we had to help each other. I took the position that any pacifist would have my full support for his right to his position and no young man would be deserted by his church if he were a conscientious objector. Part of my time was spent in testifying for such young men before their draft boards. I sometimes wished I could be an all-out militarist or an all-out pacifist. The middle ground is fair game for both sides, and the lot of the man who sees truth on both sides is not always a happy one.

I rode out to see the chaplain of Stanford University one afternoon to ask him how one began to write. Dr. Trueblood's books had helped me and I felt the first stirrings of a desire to put something between covers. His answer was fairly simple, and it went something like this: Take yourself by the seat of the pants and put that seat in a chair before a typewriter. For a certain period of every day just write. Oh, there were some other practical suggestions, I am sure, but this was the heart of it. I have thought since then that this advice is about all there is to give. Start! Half the battle is beginning, and if all the people who are going to write books someday would break this first barrier, we might not increase the number of good books, but we would decrease the number of would-be authors living in a dream world.

Those were what are sometimes referred to as "salad days." The first course had been served and it was delicious. I no longer saw The Methodist Church as a great organization bent on keeping me down. The future was wide open and I did not much care where they sent me or when they sent me. I was a minister of The Methodist Church and a preacher of the gospel. It was hard work but it was more fun than any recreation that had ever come my way. I had no staff and no secretary. My wife had not forgotten her secretarial training and she took care of my correspondence. My congregation was increasing, the church was growing, and every day I was learning something new about people and the ministry. I had the feeling that, as Churchill was to put it later, it was not the beginning of the end but the end of the beginning.

I APPRECIATE
THE HONOR . . .

TEACHING   In 1938 I was invited to teach the homiletics classes at the Pacific School of Religion in Berkeley, California. It was about fifty miles from San Jose and the church agreed to let me spend my day off on the campus. I had graduated from the institution in 1932 and it seemed like a great thing to be back as a faculty member. There began for me a four-year teaching responsibility which greatly enriched my life.

The Pacific School of Religion is on a hilltop with a magnificent view of San Francisco, the Bay, and the Golden Gate. It was a constant inspiration to me as a student, and the weekly visits to the campus renewed my youth like the eagle's. I heard a world traveler say one time that he had never seen a panorama to surpass it. In the years since, as I have wandered about the world some myself, I quite agree. To see that view in the morning, with the rising sun reflecting from San Francisco's windows, was like a vision of the Holy City. The sunsets were unforgettable as the dark mountains of Marin County contrasted the flaming color in the sky.

The site was sometimes referred to as Holy Hill. Besides the Congregational-oriented Pacific School of Religion, there were the Episcopal Seminary, the Unitarian Seminary, the Baptist Seminary, and a new Christian church all in the same general area. The University of California campus was about two blocks to the south. The Berkeley climate is ideal for study and work, being practically never too hot and nearly always fresh and stimulating.

One of my earliest experiences was to lead chapel as a new faculty member. To be numbered with the scholars was sweet indeed, and I

71

have always appreciated the friendship of men whose disciplined minds have led them into the deep places of human knowledge. To be accepted as a colleague filled me with pride which the students soon dissipated. I am a preacher primarily, but scholarship has a great attraction for me and I respect professors. Academic pursuits as ends in themselves have little appeal, and I could never be content doing research unless it promised some human betterment. But scholarship to enrich our minds and enlarge our lives seems to me one of the truly great pursuits.

The preacher gives up any possibility of being a specialized scholar. I am speaking now of the American situation where church life is nothing if it is not active. Some great books have come out of small parishes, especially in England, but the same hardly ever happens here. The pastor can be interrupted—and must be whenever there is real need for him. The professor can plot his schedule and take his sabbaticals. The preacher must know something about everything and he can never lose himself completely in one subject or in one period of time. He speaks to the present needs of men, and woe to his effectiveness if he does not know something firsthand about the way they live and how they support their families.

This does not mean that the preacher cannot be a student, for indeed he ought to squeeze the juice out of one book a day. But every time I talk with theological seminary professors, it is soon apparent how different their lives are from mine. One man told me that he was going to write a book on his next year's leave of absence. He was teaching ten hours a week and the book was to be in the field of his teaching. But he felt he simply could not get to it until he was freed completely from his teaching. His weekends were his unless he wanted to fill them, and I wondered why he had to wait for a free year.

Ask the preachers who write how they do it. We get up early in the morning and we stay up after other people are in bed. We snatch a half hour here and twenty minutes there. We scribble in hotel rooms, on planes, and during a lull between sessions of committees. Any man who waits until there is time to get in the proper mood for writing or to find the right environment will never make it in the ministry. Of course our writings usually are not the finished, scholastic contributions of the professors. Probably they must have a different situation to do what they must do and what we all expect them to do. But one thing seems clear to me; namely, that after the pressures of the pastorate, life on the seminary campus is wonderfully relaxed and leisurely.

I had never taught homiletics and knew nothing about how to start. Dr. Carl Patton, one of Congregationalism's leading preachers, had been teaching the courses and had retired because of ill health. I called on him and I shall never forget the visit which happened more than twenty-five years ago but is as clear as if it had been yesterday. He was sitting up in bed, smoking a pipe and playing solitaire. He said to me, "Young man, when you are in my condition, a few vices come in very handy." I told him how ignorant I was and how I craved help. He grinned and said, "Well, I have been teaching preaching for many years, and I've decided that if they can preach, they can preach, and if they can't, they can't, and there is nothing you can do about it." This was a low blow and he must have known it, so he went on: "But there is one thing the professor of homiletics can do. He can help the student to want to become the greatest preacher he is capable of becoming. And," he added, "that is no small accomplishment."

When, not long after that, Dr. Carl Patton died, I was present at his memorial service in the University Christian Church across from the School. It was conducted by the president of the seminary, Arthur Cushman McGiffert, Jr. As I sat there expecting the usual quiet music, the organ burst forth with a great triumphant shout. It was magnificent, and I remembered the words of the artist Burne-Jones commenting on Robert Browning's funeral: "Much would I have given for a banner or two, and much would I have given had a chorister come out of the triforium and rent the air with a trumpet." How often our so-called Christian funerals lack the essential element of rejoicing in Christ's conquest of death. Patton was a great man and it was both fear and joy to follow in his train.

My own seminary training in homiletics had consisted of a Congregational preacher, who later became my good friend, coming to the school once a week and listening to the students preach. Then he commented and we commented and that was it. I wanted to do more than that, for it has long been a mystery to me that theological schools can take the teaching of preaching so casually. After all, this is where a man will make it or lose it. If there is one single thing which defines a man's ministry more than anything else, it is preaching. But how do you teach it? I still do not know.

I prepared a series of lectures and if nothing else was accomplished, I read practically.every book that had been written on the subject. Seldom have I received any practical suggestions which were of much help from these books, but that is not their main contribution. Most preachers are such individualists that they find their own ways and not very often do they change methods of sermon preparation or delivery. Sometimes this is too bad. But these books lift one's sight and increase one's appreciation. It is always helpful to hear another man describe your profession from his point of view.

There is a place in the curriculum for lectures on preaching, I am sure. A man ought to know the background and history of his job and he ought to know what the leaders have said about it. But lectures will never produce a preacher. Here, if anywhere, a man learns by doing; and I came to believe that actual preaching is the best teaching. The discipline of preparing a sermon every week and delivering it is the way great preachers are made. John Wesley said that preaching at 5 A.M. was the best exercise in the world and was one of the secrets of his long and active life.

But preaching before critics is an ordeal for a young man. No one feels like hearing his efforts torn apart immediately after delivering his soul, and no man should be subjected to it. He feels exhausted physically, spiritually, mentally, and what he needs most of all is comfort. There seemed no other way to do it, however, and class and teacher would pounce on the poor fellow like dogs on a cornered rabbit. It was and it is cruel and inhuman. No matter how much I tried to soften the blows and express appreciation for the effort, my heart went out to these young hopefuls who would have found martyrdom not much more difficult to bear.

The great moment for the teacher is when a young man preaches his first sermon in class and you know he has it. The outline is clear and the thought is disciplined. There is an indefinable sense of drama and the material is treated freshly and with an underlying sense of excitement. You listen gladly, and while there are obvious defects and marks of immaturity and inexperience, still you know that the good Lord has found himself another preacher. This boy has been called, and one day, you would bet your life, he will be in a great pulpit and he will be a prophet unto his generation.

This does not happen very often, unfortunately. For one such experience there will be thirty discouragements. The boys mean well and they are devoted to their work, but they do not get the idea. Their stuff is mediocre, sometimes dull, and never inspiring enough to send chills up your back. Yet these men have other gifts, and some of them will make large contributions to the church. Some of them will be great pastors, or organizers, or administrators; and because the church needs so many varied gifts, there is a place for all of them. Now and again a man fools you completely. He seems headed for the top but he lacks the character to sustain him. Or a boy is a late bloomer and he comes into his own later and assumes a place of leadership. Which is to say, teaching is about as exciting a job as you are likely to find.

Teaching is hard work if the teacher feels any obligation to be interesting and stimulating. I have known men who droned through their lectures without any apparent interest in whether anybody was listening. When those brethren get tenure, a mighty blow has been struck against tomorrow. My teaching day began when I left home at 6:30 A.M. and it never ended before 7 P.M. The long day was spent in the classroom or in personal consultations. I was never sure that anything much had been accomplished, but there was no doubt that considerable energy had been expended. It was a hard day.

This experience made clear to me one thing, which at times had been somewhat blurred. I knew that God had called me to preach and that while teaching was stimulating one day a week, it was not for me a full-time profession. I have been privileged to do a little teaching in connection with my ministry in colleges and seminaries. I taught two hours a week at Nebraska Wesleyan University during my pastorate in Lincoln. I have taught short courses at Union, Garrett, and Iliff in the summer and conducted an occasional class at the Southern California School of Theology. But in spite of some very generous and urgent invitations to join graduate faculties, it has seemed to me that I did them a favor by saying no. God's will for me in this matter has seemed much clearer than in some others.

□ □ □

LINCOLN A Methodist layman from Lincoln, Nebraska, was on a business trip through California in 1942. He came to church at Palo Alto on a Sunday morning and heard me preach a sermon on the stimulating subject: "Noah Was Drunk." He was a member of the Pastoral Relations Committee of St. Paul Methodist Church, Lincoln, Nebraska, and he was looking for a possible successor to Dr. Walter Aitken, who was retiring after twenty-two years in that pulpit. A little later I had a letter from the district superintendent to see if I would consider being appointed to St. Paul Church. I wrote to Dr. Roy L. Smith, editor of the *Christian Advocate,* and asked him about the church, which was unknown to me. He told me later that he had already answered a letter from the chairman of the committee in Lincoln who had asked him concerning one Gerald Kennedy, completely unknown to the St. Paul congregation. I was properly deflated.

It developed finally to the point where it seemed best for us to visit the church. With the consent of the bishop, we went to Lincoln and talked with the committee. Looking back on the situation, I am astounded at the questions I did not ask and the problems I never saw. The bright boys today go into these situations with the thoroughness of the FBI. Usually they discover ten reasons why the church under scrutiny cannot possibly live another ten years. But I was naïve, enthusiastic, ignorant of surveys, and altogether simple. To this day I am surprised at my decision, and when the bridges were burned and the appointment was announced, I lived in a kind of unreal dream.

There were a hundred reasons why this decision was foolish. The movement was to the West and I was here already. Downtown churches are not regarded generally as opportunities for young preachers. There was no financial advantage. Yet something seemed to be urging us and I believe God nudged me. I hesitate to make this confession, for there are too many of the brethren who make a big operation out of praying for guidance when all the time a bigger salary and other fringe benefits have decided them. I find it hard to respect preachers who let their people know whenever some

76

other church shows an interest in them and then use this as a leverage for a raise in salary. No minister worth his salt will use such tactics to bargain with a church like a common huckster. Too much pious praying about such decisions always makes me suspicious.

The war was on and tires were rationed as well as gasoline. The national speed limit was forty miles per hour and the trip to Lincoln was slower than usual. It was September and the autumn is, in many ways, the best time of year in the Middle West. I remember it as one of the most relaxed weeks of my life. The work at Palo Alto was ended and the responsibilities at Lincoln had not yet found me. For Methodist preachers there is a short period between pastorates when they are free. Usually they do not come very often and they do not last very long, but they are like oases in the desert. The man under constant daily pressure has to learn how to create these brief periods deliberately. Tonight, he says to himself, I will forget the day I have just lived, and I will not give tomorrow a thought until after a good night's sleep.

St. Paul Methodist Church was Lincoln's last downtown church. It was an old brick building with not much to commend it architecturally speaking. The sanctuary was the Akron type and seated over two thousand people. The offices were downstairs with nothing modern about them. I remember that a young associate who came on my staff later was so upset with this old-fashioned arrangement that he began to agitate for a renewal plan. But my heart was not in it and the old rolltop desk hid the disorder of my work and we left it as it was. We did build a beautiful chapel in the church and made some improvements in the ladies' lounge.

I have never been as sensitive as some of my brethren to the physical conditions of worship. There is a story about Joseph Parker, the famous early minister of London's City Temple. When they decided to build a new church on Holburn Viaduct, he took the architect to a spot on the plot of ground and said, "Put the pulpit there and build a church around it." Whether the pulpit is in the center or on the side has never mattered much to me, for if a fellow has nothing to say, changing the pulpit's location does not solve any real problem. I loved St. Paul Church from the beginning and to me it will always be beautiful. If this is sentimental, it is still the way I feel.

It would be less than honest to give the impression that we were at ease from the beginning. I was homesick, as I always am in a new job. It seemed at times that nothing was right and only a fool would have left his home conference to go among strangers. There were all those empty seats to be filled every Sunday, for it is not enough to have fifteen hundred people in a place that leaves five hundred empty ones. It was my first experience in working with a staff, and that was probably harder on them than it was on me. We had forgotten how cold it can get in the winter and how hot it can be in the summer. But right from the beginning, two things saved me.

The first was my wife. She must have been as homesick as I was, but she never showed it. She never complained and she never whined. More times than I care to recall, I could have gone off the deep end had it not been for her help. A man does not deserve much personal credit for anything he does if he has that kind of support. Well, I could never say enough about her so I will say nothing more.

The second source of help was the chairman of the Pastoral Relations Committee, A. R. Talbot. He was an old man when we went to Lincoln and he died a few years later. He had been the law partner of William Jennings Bryan, and although the two men were widely separated in their political thinking, they were close friends. Nearly every Monday morning Mr. Talbot would call me on the telephone and say, "Doctor, that was another great sermon you preached yesterday. You will never know how delighted we are that you are here, and how much we love you." That word always gave me a lift and I would decide to try it another week. How can we ever be thankful enough for those friends who give us words of encouragement at the right time!

St. Paul Church was not only downtown, but it was near the campus of the University of Nebraska. I had students in my congregation and faculty members. Very often sorority and fraternity groups came to church officially and I was privileged to deal with the finest young people in the world. They were different from the sophisticates one often meets in the universities on the east and west shores. Many of them had grown up on farms out west and they had been through the depression. It was a sacrifice for their parents and for them to get to the university. They had a depth and a reality in

78

them which made the playboys look pretty cheap. It became my conviction that such as these were the hope of the future and the strength of the nation.

The people of Nebraska were wonderful too. They were humble and, unlike Californians, they did very little boasting. They played down their climate and their land and seemed almost embarrassed if you paid a compliment to the state. They were sometimes on the conservative side, but there was never the slightest attempt to limit my freedom. I did not find the reactionary religious attitudes that I found later in some parts of the Northwest. They were loyal and dependable. In my book, they are the salt of the earth and any preacher is blessed who has been in their midst. My six years in Lincoln were a high point in my ministry.

The church in Lincoln had an established place in the community. St. Paul had such a large sanctuary that it was used for commencements, concerts, and public meetings. I still meet people who tell me they graduated in St. Paul Church. The leaders of the city were churchmen, and a survey of my service club showed that its members belonged to a church and most of them were active. I have never been in a place which took me into the center of civic affairs as they did in Lincoln. I was on the board of the Community Chest, president of the Council of Social Agencies, member of the mayor's committee on youth, etc., etc. I joined the Junior Chamber of Commerce and made quite an impression by the way it was done. The executive secretary said he wanted to talk to me about it and would appreciate ten minutes on a certain day. I told him if he would meet me at 6:15 A.M., in my office, I would talk with him. When he found I was not fooling, he came at the appointed hour and then talked about it all over town. Men who get to work early when they do not have to are an anomaly to most people.

The church gave me considerable freedom. I had a gentleman's agreement with the Pastoral Relations Committee not to take more than two Sundays away from my pulpit during the year, in addition to a month's vacation in the summer. But during the week I was at liberty to travel and preach about the country. It seems as if I gave high-school commencement speeches in every town in Nebraska. One night I might be speaking where the class had four graduates, and the next night it might include four hundred. The class mottoes were taken very seriously. Some of them, such as "The Elevator to Success Is Not Working; Take the Stairs," were quite impressive. My wife and I more than once drove all night getting to an appointment. Forgetting that winter in Nebraska is different from winter in California, we sometimes were caught in blizzards. They were great years, and when a man has exciting work and good health, he ought never to complain.

Looking back on that period, I guess I worked pretty hard. I started at 5:30 A.M. and was hardly ever finished before 10 P.M. Every night there was a meeting of some kind, except Saturday evening which we reserved for ourselves. A young man who came on my staff asked me, after he had been with us several weeks, if he could take a day off next week. It never dawned on me until then that we had no days off and we had made no provision for it. The office was open each day, although it closed Saturday and Sunday afternoons. Saturday afternoon was one of my most productive times of study. My secretary was a girl who had come to work for the church with the same dedication men should exhibit when they enter the ministry. Overtime meant nothing and I doubt if the church members ever fully appreciated what they owed her. But I did.

Preachers grow under the stimulation of great congregations. In this I have been more than fortunate and the St. Paul congregation inspired and demanded the very best a man had to give. It was one of the great pulpits and there was hardly any carping criticism or smallness of spirit. Churches take on character with the passing years and achieve something closely akin to personality. Now and again you find a congregation made mean and small by its leadership. Then there are the bargainers who want to get as much as possible for as little as possible. St. Paul Church stands in my mind as the great example of a church which makes the ministry joy and fulfillment.

I must pay my respects to the men of the Nebraska Annual Conference. They might have looked upon a fellow from California with considerable suspicion. Who was I to be given such a church in the conference when they had borne the heat and burdens of the day? I have heard of situations where conferences hold a man at arm's length if he is a transfer from the outside. But those brethren gave me a warm welcome and took me into the fellowship immediately. In a short time, it seemed to me that I had lived in Nebraska all my life. In 1944 the brethren elected me a delegate to the Jurisdictional Conference and in 1948 I was elected on the first ballot to head the General Conference delegation. No one can ever quite know what that meant to me. Ah, those wonderful years in Nebraska!

EPISCOPACY On Friday, July 6, 1948, I was attending a picnic in Pioneer Park, Lincoln, Nebraska. We had a group of ex-GI's and their wives in our church, and every other week we met with them for some recreation. They were university students trying to make up for lost time, and older than most campus young people. After our potluck dinner we played baseball and I got stuck behind the bat. A foul tip caught me on the finger and broke it, though I did not know it at the time. We broke up early because some of the couples had children, and my wife and I decided to attend an outdoor movie. We were opening the front door of the parsonage about 11 P.M. when the telephone rang. It was Western Union with a wire from Seattle, Washington, informing me that I had been elected a bishop on the thirteenth ballot by the Western Jurisdiction of The Methodist Church. A little later two friends called and confirmed the wire.

Nothing except marriage ever changed my life so completely. For one thing, it came almost as a complete surprise. The afternoon before, one of my friends from California had telephoned to say that my name was in the picture and that I had better make up my mind what I would do if elected. I told him that such an eventuality was far-fetched and that when the real decision had to be made, the Western Jurisdiction would not elect a man living outside. That was my honest conviction and the whole matter was put out of my mind.

When The Methodist Church achieved union in 1939, it was divided into geographical sections called "jurisdictions." These divisions had the power to elect their bishops, and it never seemed likely to me that they would overlook men close at hand who were members of the lodge, so to speak, in favor of an outsider whose work and loyalties were elsewhere. But the Western Jurisdiction, less tradition bound than some, had done just that.

My wife and I walked around the block in the warm, humid midnight and tried to decide what to do next. We called the airlines and managed to get reservations late on Saturday for Seattle via San Francisco. Then I called the president of Nebraska Wesleyan University and found he could and would preach for me on Sunday. Sleep was uneven and full of wild dreaming, partly because my finger had swelled up and hurt. The next morning the doctor found it was broken, put a splint on, and bandaged it.

We arrived in San Francisco on Sunday morning and had time for breakfast with relatives and friends. Our arrival in Seattle was at a different airport than welcoming friends had anticipated, which took extra time. We were a little late for the consecration service at University Methodist Church, which is not the way for a Methodist preacher to begin any undertaking. I thought that one or two of the elder bishops were a little irritated by this slight delay though it might have been my imagination. The service was most impressive but it was all like a dream to me, and to this day it is blurred like some of Turner's seascapes. There was a reception with a long line, the first of many. There were congratulations and a warm welcome.

I had been assigned to the Portland Area, which included the states of Washington, Oregon, Idaho, and the Territory of Alaska. My predecessor was the late Bishop Bruce Baxter whose untimely death about a year before my election had saddened the whole church. I have never followed a man more universally beloved. During the interim, retired bishop Francis J. McConnell had been serving the Portland Area. He was a great man and one of my heroes. I walked with him into the room where the ministers and laymen of my new area were waiting. "Bishop," I said, "I know nothing about this business and I hope we can spend a little time together tomorrow so that you can give me some guidance and advice." "Oh," he an-

82

swered, "I am taking a train in about an hour. There is a fellow over east who wants to move but he will tell you about it. You will be all right. Good luck." That was my initiation.

The next morning, we flew down the coast to San Francisco. It is a beautiful flight when it is clear, and the day was sunny and bright. The mountains loomed up on the left with now and then a great, snow-covered peak standing out against the sky. Below and to the right, there was the coastline and the expanse of the Pacific. Strange that the flight and the scenery are so much clearer in my mind than the consecration service. We were met in San Francisco by Mrs. Kennedy's parents, and we spent three weeks at their home in Modesto. It was always a haven of rest for me, but this time it was a place to work. I was in the midst of preparing the Peyton Lectures, to be delivered the next February at Southern Methodist University. I knew it was now or never, and the book which became *The Lion and the Lamb* was written in those days. The inscription reads: "This is for Grace and Ray," who were my mother-in-law and father-in-law and as dear to me as any two people in the world.

We had to go back to Lincoln to arrange for moving, get the car, and preach one more sermon. I went on ahead and when the train arrived in Omaha one night, there were people marching up and down the platform with placards. They were my secretary, my associate pastor, and some friends. One sign read: "All Lincoln is Proud." I have been blessed with staff members who were loyal and efficient, and it has been a great satisfaction to have found some of my most meaningful and lasting friendships among them.

On Sunday morning, as I entered the pulpit, the whole congregation rose. I was so startled I did not know what to do. The chairman of the Official Board had arranged it as a courtesy and it symbolized in one moment the loyalty and affection of a great church for a minister who wished he knew some way to express his thanks. I doubt if there is anything just like this experience in the whole world. A bishop never finds it, though there are other experiences almost as wonderful. But if a pastor has been with a congregation for a number of years, there develops a bond which is eternal. They have been together in the greatest enterprises of human life and they are bound to each other by experiences and memories. Listen to the tone of voice when a faithful layman talks about his pastor. Catch a preacher in a quiet moment when he talks about his people. Then you know you have entered a holy place where a divine relationship has been shared.

The trip west was not the first long automobile trip we had taken, but it was one of the best. It was autumn and we went by way of the Grand Tetons and the Jackson Hole country. I remember the changing leaves in Idaho and the flocks of sheep being brought down to lower country. Once again, it was that neutral period when the old job was finished and the new one had not yet started.

Getting settled is always a nuisance and my predecessor had been content with a room in Portland's First Methodist Church which was used on Sundays by a Sunday-school class. A layman managed to get me two rooms in what later was called Jackson Tower and I was in business. We rented a very satisfactory home in King's Heights on the west side of Portland and from my bedroom window I could see Mount Adams, Mount Hood, and Mount St. Helens. There is no more wonderful country than the Northwest, with its great trees, lofty mountains, and beautiful rivers. A man from Arizona once remarked that he never knew until he moved to Oregon how much water added to a river.

We were strangers in a strange land. Our closest friends were in California and we had to get acquainted with laymen and ministers. This was more difficult than when I was a minister of a local church. It had never been so clear to me before that a minister immediately has a large number of friends ready to receive him. This is a good thing, for most of our preachers move about considerably during their lifetimes. But as a bishop I was in a different situation with no local habitation and a parish that extended over three states and a territory which later became the largest state in the union. There was little opportunity for close, personal relations with laymen at first, and I missed having lunch with my men and discussing church affairs. The ministers hesitated to call as they would have done had I been another minister moving into their neighborhood. For the first time in many a day, we were lonesome.

Part of it was caused by an almost total ignorance of what being a bishop meant. I had never been a district superintendent, which is excellent training for the episcopacy. I had never sat in a cabinet meeting and knew nothing about making appointments or dealing with church pastoral relations committees. My own relations with bishops had been rather formal and occasional. You could hardly imagine a greater change than to take a minister, suddenly elect him a bishop, and then, without further training or teaching, expect him to start exercising the duties of his office. New jobs are overwhelming anyway until you find the things that are essential and the matters that may be pushed aside. It is rather terrifying to face a million details and not know which ones are not to be neglected at any cost. As a result, a man tries to give every request his full attention and longs for the old days when he had some control over his job.

I remember my first Sunday as a bishop. We went to Tacoma and spent Saturday afternoon and evening with the president of the University of Puget Sound. Sunday morning I preached at one of the churches and had dinner with the minister and his family. There was a new sanctuary to be consecrated in the afternoon, and then it was suggested that it would be much appreciated if we stopped by to congratulate a minister and his wife who were celebrating their fiftieth wedding anniversary. Next was the consecration of a new parsonage with a choir singing "Bless This House" slightly off key. I preached in the evening and started home after 9 P.M. I should have said that it rained most of the day and it poured all the way to Portland. When I finally fell into bed I prayed one short prayer: "O Lord, must I do this the rest of my life?"

A little later on, two different churches sounded me out about resigning the episcopal office and going back into the pastorate. I would have agreed in a moment if I had followed my own inclination. But the Portland Area had been without leadership for some time and there was an obligation to finish out at least a quadrennium. By that time, things were different and I had changed my mind. Today I find it very difficult to feel sorry for myself, and the episcopacy has been an increasing joy. It is full of paradoxes and contrasts and just about the most exciting calling in the world. I would trade

85

salaries with some men I know, but I would not trade jobs with any man.

The episcopal office in The Methodist Church is unique. For one thing it is an *office* and not an *order,* which puts it closer to the New Testament episcopacy. I was a traveling elder elected to ordain young men and appoint my brethren to their churches. To do the work of a bishop, I had been given certain authority which, as one of my colleagues put it, would be no greater than a man deserved, no matter what the *Discipline* said. Mine was the responsibility of being a pastor to the pastors, a leader of an area, a preacher of the gospel. I found I stood as a bridge between laymen and preachers to interpret one to the other and make clear our common tasks. It is a task to shrink the ego and drive a man to his knees.

THIS
GREAT
RESPONSIBILITY . . .

COUNCIL   Away back in 1947, my first book, *His Word Through Preaching,* was published. One of the chapters was "The Tension of Meeting." The theme of that chapter was that Christianity is the experience of being confronted—of meeting—God. The church has tended to put an "s" on that word and make its life a never-ending, continuous procession of meetings. I am sure that no body of Christians is more guilty of this than the Methodists. If meetings could save the world, we would have accomplished it long ago.

The time came in my own ministry when it did not seem I could stand it any longer. Those endless discussions about generalities and abstractions nearly drove me mad. Who shall save us from those public gatherings where you eat a poor meal, talk boring nonsense with people as bored as you (there are some striking exceptions to this), listen to a speaker who has something to say but does not know how to say it, or else has nothing to say but tries to cover it up with glibness and shallow cleverness! Endless committee meetings designed to waste an evening, a lunch hour, a late afternoon, are a nightmare to any man aware of the value of time. A friend of mine put it very well: "If the children of Israel had depended on a committee," he said, "they would still be in Egypt." But I digress.

I started out to say that when I learned that the Council of Bishops met twice a year, I was filled with dismay. How could a fellow stand it to spend four days in the autumn and again in the spring discussing ecclesiastical business affairs? For I might as well admit that I took a rather distant view of bishops in general, mainly because I had never known them personally. A few of them I had admired from a distance, and James C. Baker and William C. Martin I had served under and loved.

I have always regarded Bishop Baker as my father in the gospel, for in the early days of my ministry he was my chief pastor. His sympathies were always with young men, and he began visiting the theological seminaries to talk with students about California before the other brethren came around to the same practice. Then, when everybody started doing it, the students began to think the bishops were bidding against one another and it took all the fun out of it. In those days the San Francisco Area included the whole state of California, plus Nevada, Arizona, and the Hawaiian Islands. Not on the basis of any financial advantage, but with the challenge of an exciting frontier, Bishop Baker enlisted some of the most promising young preachers from all over the country. The area was divided in 1948, and as bishop of the southern half of it since 1952, I am the happy inheritor of some of my predecessor's wise plans and policies. Bishop Baker was always on the front line of the social applications of Christianity. I can remember yet a conference of preachers he addressed when I was in the first year of my ministry, when he urged us to speak our word without fear. It is not a common experience for young preachers to hear their bishop encourage them to be more courageous on controversial social issues. The thrill of that memory has warmed my heart for many years, and it is kindled anew every time Bishop Baker (now retired) and I are together.

Bishop William C. Martin had the same great quality. He presided over the Nebraska Conference during the years of my ministry in Lincoln. From the former southern part of the church, he soon became admired as much in the north. He is a Christian statesman with nothing petty in his nature, and always ecumenical in his outlook. Like all the other men of the Nebraska Conference, I loved him and we consented to his leaving us to go to the Dallas-Fort Worth Area in 1948 with great reluctance.

But most of the bishops were only names and I assumed that most of them must be different from the ones I knew. I went to the first meeting with suspicion and resolved to at least keep my mouth shut. I did not even know that the man sitting across the table from me was Arthur Moore, which indicates the extent of my ignorance. But I have never entered the company of a group of men who so quickly changed suspicion into trust and transformed a reluctant spirit into

90

an eager expectation. The fellowship of the Council of Bishops has been to me one of the most precious experiences of my life. I have missed only two meetings, and nothing preventable keeps me away from our sessions. There are a number of things a man elected to the episcopacy must give up, but the experience of being in the council more than makes up for practically all of them.

As I think about it, the wonderful truth is that we all love one another. I do not want to put this on any sentimental basis, for it is something very deep. I know there are conflicting temperaments; and now and then two of the brethren may aspire for the same goal and only one of them attains it. We differ, but it came to me not long ago that there is not a single member of the council I dislike. It would be my honest opinion that this testimony would be unanimous and that not a single bishop would ask for help from any other bishop without receiving it in full measure.

There was one brother who was—let us face it—pompous. He could not make an announcement without making it sound like an oration. When he was retired, he never missed a meeting and he spoke on many subjects. Whenever he took over, there was an almost audible groan from the brethren, though he spoke as long as he pleased without interruption if not with complete attention. This, by the way, is an unwritten law of the council and no one ever moves the previous question. I came to have a real affection for that man, for he was naturally pompous and it was not an acquired trait at all. He had been born that way. Strangely enough, when we talked together from time to time, I found a real human being underneath the veneer of pomposity and I discovered a wisdom which was deep and wide.

When I first entered the council there were thirty-seven active bishops in this country and now there are forty-three. At an average meeting there will be present in addition about ten retired men and perhaps a half dozen from overseas. I doubt that you could find in any group of the same size more rugged individuals who are less impressed with any single way of doing anything. Whether such men are elected to the office or whether the office creates such men, I do not know. The members of the fellowship are not organization men full of togetherness, but men who have found their unity in a cause and a purpose beyond them all. It is tempting to stop for a moment and exhort on this theme. Unity does not come about by bludgeoning people into silence and conformity or by pasting labels on those disapproved of by the self-appointed guardians of orthodoxy; it comes about through freedom and the diversity of different interpretations of the common cause. Thus endeth the lesson!

There is a wide divergence of opinion in The Methodist Council of Bishops. Some of the brethren are very conservative and see the church as called to deal mainly with the individual and his inner religion. They are troubled when they are called upon to join in any pronouncement on a contemporary issue. If there is to be change of any kind, they want it to come gradually and, if possible, imperceptibly. These men are sincere in believing that along this path lies the best route for Christians, and in the long run they believe this is the road to the Kingdom.

There are, on the other side, bishops who are in the forefront of all attempts to make the gospel relevant to the present situation. They are not impressed by threats from either the right or the left, and neither rich man nor poor man can swerve them from their course. I have listened to some of the most fearless and prophetic utterances on the floor of the council. The Methodist Church ought to know that its Council of Bishops represents the two main strains of its tradition; namely, personal piety and social concern.

In between these two positions most of the brethren find themselves. Sometimes the majority will favor a conservative position and sometimes it will proclaim a liberal point of view. There is much debate and a careful weighing of all the elements in the situation before the council commits itself. In the beginning, I became restless and impatient with so much refining and defining. But with the passing years I have more appreciation for the value of this process, although impatience still plagues me more than it should. I am convinced that when and if the council can unanimously adopt a statement, it is as near being a fair statement of the position of The Methodist Church as we are likely to get.

There is a vast amount of experience in the council, which means there is considerable wisdom to be found there also. These men have been dealing with laymen, preachers, secretaries, conference programs. They have learned what will work and what will be scuttled. New bishops soon learn to respect this experience, and very early in my episcopal ministry I began to consult my brethren before trying anything very new in my area. Now and again some apparently harmless proposition is put before us and we are ready to approve it. Then some elderly statesman takes the floor to describe the hidden traps in this idea and he will probably give illustrations from his own experience. Usually we either modify it or forget it.

I came into the council two quadrenniums after unification. The three main branches of The Methodist Church were united in 1939 with bishops from the north and south joined together in a single body, and with two men elected by the former Methodist Protestant Church. There were real problems to deal with and the times demanded patience and wisdom. I am convinced that one of the main factors in bringing the united church through its growing pains with reasonable ease was the Council of Bishops. These men knew one another, trusted one another, and could interpret the hopes and fears of all parts of the church. In the little more than twelve years I have been a bishop, the unity between north and south, east and west, has grown and become firm. My own friendships, for example, have no geographical or cultural boundaries. I feel as much at home in one place as another, and my companions in the council who are very dear to me are from Mississippi, Tennessee, Maryland, Texas, Oklahoma, Indiana, the Northwest, New England. In all the days ahead, it seems clear to me that the council will continue to be a balance wheel and a center of unity.

At the close of our meeting in Boston in the spring of 1961, I handed over the president's gavel to my successor, Bishop Paul Martin from Houston. After adjournment I walked around the block with my wife, who asked me why I was so quiet. Well, I had been thinking of the great men who had enriched my life in the Council of Bishops. I remember men like Francis J. McConnell, Edwin Hughes, Charles Flint. And I felt sad at the retirement of Bromley Oxnam, Arthur Moore, Frank Smith, Earl Ledden. Bishop Oxnam had been at the meeting and so had Frank Smith, though he had left early, and Arthur Moore had been unable to attend. It came to me how much these men and many others had come to mean to me personally and how great was their contribution to the church. A pioneer Oregon Methodist in referring to conference leaders and Bishop Matthew Simpson said, "Their ware Jiants in the Oregon Conference in Those days." In my few years' experience, I have known giants in the council.

□ □ □

PERSONAL   I want to speak of some personal things in the Council of Bishops. This is hard to do without being stilted or mawkish. Yet I have long felt a desire to share some of these experiences with others and courage has silenced prudence. Strange that what we feel most profoundly is so often the most difficult to communicate. The preacher finds this true in every sermon. What he would really like to say he can hardly find words to express. We talk glibly only when we are on the surface.

One of the significant features of our spring meetings is the memorial service when we remember and pay honor to the bishops and bishops' wives who have left us during the year. There have been some high moments which none of us will ever forget and these meetings are like family gatherings rather than formal services.

Some years ago when Bishop Edwin Holt Hughes died, Bishop Francis J. McConnell spoke about his longtime friend and colleague. The two men were different in so many ways, yet there was a strong bond of friendship between them. Bishop McConnell made us weep and laugh, and my impression was that this was the way a Christian funeral service should be. When I compare it with the professionally sweet, sentimental, sick way we conduct most of our funerals, I wish that every Methodist could have been present. Bishop McConnell spoke of Ed Hughes' last illness and of a call he made on him. Bishop Hughes had said that he had dreamed he was dead and surrounded by his district superintendents. "Ed," said McConnell, "that was no vision of paradise." None of us will ever forget the conclusion of the remarks. "I had wanted to see Ed Hughes at the last meeting of the council we both attended," said Francis McConnell. "But I arrived late and he had left early." Then he paused a moment. "Oh, well," he said, "it can wait a while." And in that moment, the glorious faith in eternal life was real to me in a new and wonderful way.

We had one service in which there were seven persons to be memorialized. It was agreed that each man would speak for seven minutes, and all lived up to their promise save one. He spoke twenty-seven minutes and one of my colleagues murmured as he sat down: "And he did it without any notes!" The next day in our business session, one of the brethren was quoting something and he said, "Let's see. Who said that yesterday? Was it Bishop ——————?" (naming the one who had spoken so long the night before). "Probably," said Bishop Hughes drily. We have a wide range of give and take without anyone taking offense.

There is a rule that retired bishops may speak but may not vote in the council, which was in the *Discipline* before I became a member. This has been challenged, but it has been declared constitutional on two different occasions by the Judicial Council. I do not know the reasoning back of the rule, but I suspect it was a feeling that the retired brethren might at any one time represent a considerable block of voting power. It may have been feared that this would put a heavy weight of conservatism in the balance. I doubt that this would be true, for my observation is that there is as wide a diversity of opinion among the retired bishops as there is among the effective ones.

In 1951, for example, we were working on the Episcopal Address for the General Conference of 1952, and the question was raised concerning unordained men administering the communion. I was very much against any change and took my stand with John Wesley, who never consented to allow his local preachers to give the sacrament to their people. But Bishop Herbert Welch was just as committed to the other position and thought we should be guided by practical considerations and not by tradition. Bishop Welch was then 89 years old and had been retired since 1936. I was the youngest member of the council.

On one occasion, we had a long discussion and thought we were ready to vote, when a retired brother took the floor and held forth for some time. A bishop whom I shall not name whispered, "Let's take away the right to talk and restore the right to vote." Actually, it is more important to have the privilege of speaking than voting, and we do not adopt anything important unless there is a common sense of the meeting. But voting is a courtesy I wish we might restore to retired bishops. The council is the only body to which a bishop belongs in The Methodist Church, for he is not a member of a church or of a conference. At the General Conference he does not even preside after he is retired. More and more it seems to me that the voting privilege in the council should be given to all bishops.

One of the important responsibilities given to us is the preparation and presentation of the Episcopal Address before the General Conference. This is supposed to be a rather complete document dealing with the state of the church, the state of society, and the state of the world. No one present is likely to forget the length of the 1952 address delivered by Bishop Paul Kern. We were working on it late one night and there seemed to be a stalemate in regard to our statement on integration. What the large majority wanted was quite obvious, but a minority was holding out for a less forthright statement. I was tired and discouraged and had the feeling that bitterness had invaded our fellowship.

The next morning Bishop A. Frank Smith asked me to have breakfast with him. "Now Jerry," he said, "I saw how troubled you were last night. But you do not need to feel upset. We will work out the difference and those two fellows who argued so loud and long will continue to be the best of friends. They have been spittin' through the same crack for years." And he was right. Probably the statement finally voted did not please anyone completely, but it represented the meeting place of men with honest differences, and no trace of lasting bitterness remained.

We have a lot of fun in the council. It is unusual to have two brothers as bishops but such is our situation with Bishop A. Frank Smith, now retired, and Bishop W. Angie Smith. For all his long episcopal career, Frank Smith presided over the Houston Area, and since his election in 1944 Angie Smith has been in the Oklahoma-New Mexico Area. One of the most enjoyable features of our meetings has been the exchanges between these brothers. It is always insulting, sharp, satirical and full of laughs. One of the men from overseas was quite perturbed at his first meeting when this exchange hit him for the first time. He thought we had a real feud going but he soon learned, as the rest of us knew already, that there is a bond of brotherly love and affection between Frank and Angie which is beautiful to behold.

I remember that Bishop Angie Smith was bragging one time that the Indian Conference had given him a beautiful saddle. He pointed out that when Frank had presided over it they had only given him a hat. Frank replied that they gave each of them a present for the end they favored most. They both have the gift of pungent speech and some of their expressions should be broadcast to enrich the language. Regarding a preacher who looked fine but did not work very hard, one of them said he was "all mane and tail." Commenting on a rivalry between strong conference leaders, their word was that there were "too many he-coons in the small holler." Wonderful!

The stories from the southern brethren in particular relieve the tensions and give fresh perspectives. Bishop Arthur Moore was a master at bringing in the right story at the right time. Seldom did he repeat and always he was to the point. I shall regret forever that I was not at the conference when Arthur Moore retired and Frank Smith spoke about him. These men never are boring and I could listen to them by the hour with pleasure. And with their humor is a graciousness that those of us from the north can well emulate.

One of the great inspirations to all of us is Methodism's senior bishop, Herbert Welch. He was born on November 7, 1862, and is as sharp and keen as ever. He speaks very little in the council, but when he does speak, we listen with great interest and appreciation. From the long perspective of a century, he is not taken in easily, but there is not the slightest impression of a man living in the past. When we had our induction service for the new bishops in 1960, I asked him to speak and his words rang with wisdom, confidence, and hope. Whenever I receive a note from him, it is a high point of the day, for it is always encouraging and full of light. When an old Methodist patriarch in England was ninety-eight years old, Dr. Roy L. Smith said to him, "Doctor, I hope to see you celebrate your one hundredth birthday." "Well," said the old man, "you look as if you are in pretty good shape. I think you'll make it." I remember very clearly the night that Bishop Welch said the same thing to me.

Bishop Earl Ledden is our musician and he always plays our hymns in the devotional services. When he was president of the council, he conducted the devotions and asked Bishop Richard Raines to play the piano. Dick Raines is quite competent, but when hymn 417 in the *Methodist Hymnal* was announced he said, "We will sing number 416, 'Blest Be the Tie that Binds.' I can play that one better." Well, we sang it all right, but then Bishop Ledden compared the two hymns stanza by stanza and showed how superior Charles Wesley's was to the more familiar one. I am impressed by the varied gifts of my colleagues, and to be with them has been an education in itself.

Immediately after my election in 1948, I began to worry about the first conferences I would have to conduct. What happens and what has to be done? Just what is the bishop's responsibility? In the midst of my concern, Bishop Fred Corson of Philadelphia said that if I wanted him to do it, he would fly out to Idaho and be with me as I presided over the sessions. I accepted his gracious offer and felt safe with him at my right hand. In the passing years, that deed of kindness has come to symbolize the Council of Bishops for me. It was a real sacrifice to leave his work and spend a week in a small western conference, and it was just plain kindness. When, in the spring of 1961, two new bishops asked me to be with them at their first conferences, I cleared my schedule and went with Bishop W. Kenneth Pope to the North Arkansas Conference and with Bishop Kenneth Copeland to the Nebraska Conference.

How quickly the years pass. When I was forty and getting ready to settle down and enjoy middle age, I was elected a bishop and everybody began talking about how young I was. So I had to play the part and it was like starting all over again as a youth. Now the great men of the council are retiring and those of us who yesterday were novices today are old-timers. I look at the pictures taken a few years ago and am saddened to note how many have died. It gives me an empty feeling to realize how quickly the council changes and how fast they come and go. But every night I thank God that it is my privilege to have this experience, and I am comforted by looking forward to seeing them all again one day.

98

ADMINISTRATION   Administration has never been one of my favorite pastimes. When my longtime friend and successor at Palo Alto told me that he enjoyed putting on financial campaigns and organizing programs, I was shocked. But there are men with great gifts in this field who find it fun—which is probably one of the main reasons they do it so well. But like it or not, every preacher has to learn how to do it, for his is the final responsibility. Yet to this day, the hours spent in the details of administering the program never have the sparkle of the hours spent in study or sermon preparation.

I think most anyone can learn to be a pretty good administrator. It demands patience and a careful planning of many details. It calls for some tact in working with people, and I suppose some leadership is involved. But it is not an activity demanding genius, nor is it like preaching where so much has to be given and where the essential thing cannot be attained by effort alone. I knew two presidents of great department stores in Lincoln and it was a marvel to me how they could know what was going on in such establishments. One of them said to me one day, "It is very simple. You just get the right men for the department heads, and let them alone."

There is something to that idea in any successful administration. The man who has to do everything himself will not be able to handle a far-flung enterprise. Neither will the man who has no judgment about other men's abilities and qualities. I have a friend who is a genius at keeping his hand on all the affairs of his church. He had an associate pastor with some ideas of his own and some wondered how they would get along together. After a year I inquired of a layman close to the situation. "They are doing fine," reported the layman. "The associate now has the key to the coke machine." This was a testimony to the growth of mutual confidence.

I have had an increasing sense of the importance of good administration. Whether a man is head of a social agency, or a school, or a business, or a church, amazingly little is accomplished by the brilliant talker who does not know how to consolidate his ideas and implement his dreams. This, perhaps, is more the case in the United

States than elsewhere, at least so far as the church is concerned. Any institution which accepts the role of being relevant to society will demand able administrators. The secret of the lasting quality of John Wesley's ministry was his skill in organization and his sense of the importance of administration.

The thing that worried me the most about the episcopacy was whether or not a man could continue to be a preacher, a student, a writer. At the service of induction for the new bishops in 1952, one of the older brethren held forth for some time about the bishop's lack of opportunity for reading and studying. Four years later, Bishop F. Gerald Ensley, nephew of Bishop Francis J. McConnell, said to his uncle, "They tell me that a bishop never has time to read a book." The old man gave that quizzical look so familiar to those who knew him. "Jerry," he said, "some of those fellows did not read any books before they were elected bishops."

That was a wise observation, for it implied that the office does not change radically the natures and behavior of men. If a man has been a student before his election, he remains one. If he has been a preacher who took his preparation seriously, he will not change as a bishop. If he wrote books before, he will write books after. Perhaps it takes more will power and discipline to cultivate the intellectual life as a bishop than it does as a pastor. The program is even more impossible and a man's time is even less his own. One has to learn to study on the run and a regular schedule is an impossibility. There is the added temptation to use old sermons and allow other demands to crowd out preaching preparation.

I find myself doing my work in blocks. Last week I may have been riding the ranges and running an area program. But this week I can have two days for recharging the intellectual battery and I must read my head off from early morning until late at night. This is not as satisfactory as to have all one's mornings for study, but it will have to do. More than ever before, it is necessary to have the long look and plan far ahead, for several demands have a habit of arriving at the same hour.

It does not seem to me that episcopal administration is much more difficult than the administration of a large church. This depends partly on how many conferences are involved and the geographical size of the area. But if you have well-organized conferences and an adequate staff to help carry the administrative load, a bishop can be something besides an administrator, as he should be. Much of his success in this field will depend on his ability to appoint outstanding district superintendents who can carry responsibilities. Of course there are many things which are demanded of the bishop himself, but anything that can be done by others should be done by competent people.

The main burden of the pastor's administration is his inability to get away from it. One cantankerous layman can cause all kinds of trouble, mostly because he is always there. Everywhere the preacher turns, there stands that troublemaker, constantly draining off the preacher's nervous energy. As one of my colleagues one time said, "The Methodist Church polity makes it possible to move preachers when necessary, and it is too bad we cannot now and then move a layman." But the bishop deals with his problems and then returns to his office. He does not have to live with them at close hand. Of course some of these fellows write letters, but that is no problem if the bishop has a large wastebasket.

One of the main dilemmas in maintaining the episcopal office is to be a leader, an individual, and at the same time to remember you are responsible for a large institution. In the beginning, I was in the habit of speaking my mind on most any issue because it was hardly ever quoted beyond the local community. I learned that the office carries a certain authority, and people have the idea that the bishop's word is the voice of the church. Most Methodists know that only the General Conference speaks for The Methodist Church, but there are always a few reactionaries who insist that the episcopal office must be mute unless it is saying what they agree with completely.

Each man has to find his own way through this difficulty. I try to respect all honest differences of opinion and to make it crystal clear that when I express an opinion, it may be a poor thing, but it is mine own. A few years ago I became honorary chairman of a committee organized to elect two new people on the Los Angeles School Board. Everywhere I traveled I had heard our Board of Education laughed at for its attitude toward the United Nations and toward freedom of opinion anywhere. Robert Hutchins was reported to have said that

101

every city has its fringe groups, but in Los Angeles they elect them to the school board. I entered the battle reluctantly and our candidates won by substantial majorities, though every newspaper was on the side of the status quo. Their favorite attack was that the church had no right to be mixed up in politics. Well, I was not the church, but a citizen of no mean city. I made it as clear as possible that I was acting as an individual and it was a matter of conscience, which is an uncomfortable thing to possess. Even more than a pastor, a bishop has to consider carefully his role as a citizen and as a churchman. But I am not willing to concede that the office frees a man from the responsibility and the privilege of his convictions.

Another dilemma is the conflict between a bishop's relationship to his own area and to the church at large. Methodist bishops serve on national boards and commissions and most of their meetings are in the East. We have fewer bishops in the Western Jurisdiction than in most of the others, so that each man has more assignments of this kind. There is an obligation to serve the whole church and it is important. But if you have high-powered programs going in your own area, it is impossible to find the time to attend all the meetings requiring your presence. If you fail to attend, you are not properly representing your part of the church. But if you attend them all, you are away too much. Most of us decide what is most important in our own judgment, and then leave undone the things for which there is no time. I feel my obligation to serve on some of the national boards, though I would be glad to have others do it if they would.

I read that President Truman had a little sign on his desk which said, "The buck stops here." I have felt that about my own responsibility many times when finally the decision has to be made. It is poor administration to refuse to make a decision in the hope that time will take care of it. Time often makes it worse and changes a minor problem into a major catastrophe. Churches may have affection for men who drift but they do not respect them, for they know instinctively that such men can cause much damage. When all the facts are in, then a man had better make up his mind.

There are a great many booby traps along the episcopal trail, however. I have made some terrible mistakes because the whole picture was not clear. Both laymen and preachers come to the bishop with words of desperation so that he feels something must be done at once. It will not wait another day. Then you discover after you have acted that you had only a partial picture and, in any case, it was a prejudiced point of view. It would have been much better to have waited. There are so many things in this business that seem to be immediately good but sow the seeds for future trouble. This is the place where there is no substitute for experience, and that is a product not attained easily or quickly. Every area assigned a new bishop needs to pray for him an extra portion of grace and for themselves, the gift of patience.

The Methodist Church has spelled out the rights and duties of laymen, preachers, district superintendents, and bishops. This pattern has nearly two hundred years of experience behind it, and the whole procedure is reviewed every four years by the General Conference. It is important that the bishop should not overstep his prerogatives and it is important that others should not overstep theirs. The man to make this clear to everybody concerned is the bishop.

The Methodist Church has given its bishops life tenure and authority to do the work that has been committed unto them. We do not have to curry favor or play a political game. We are expected to labor with an eye single to the service of God and to the good of the church. Our administration should be firm, fair, and open. Bromley Oxnam told me one time that a bishop will offend ten per cent of the men every Annual Conference so that in ten years, everybody will hate him. But thanks to the graciousness of Methodist people, it does not usually work out that way. Indeed, even the man who does not find it his first choice may find administration a means of self-discipline and even grace.

LET ME BE FRANK...

CABINET   For all my ministry the term "Bishop's Cabinet" was just a phrase. I never appeared before this group and I never saw it in action. It was never clear to me just what went on at its sessions and I had the young preacher's suspicion of all its procedures and accomplishments. To me it was a part of Methodism's machinery, although its necessity was never apparent. I have decided that if it was possible to be so wrong in one case, a fellow ought to be suspicious of all his conclusions. You would be shocked to learn how many places there are in our church where nothing happens unless the district superintendent makes it happen. This is why so many church organizations move toward more supervision and why the district superintendency of The Methodist Church is one of its signs of genius.

As a new bishop, I found myself in immediate and close contact with the district superintendents of the Oregon, Idaho, and Pacific Northwest conferences. They used to be called "presiding elders," which in some ways was a better name. Each of them has to supervise a district which often takes in a large territory. Later on, one of my superintendents covered nearly all of Arizona, while another one was responsible for part of the city of Los Angeles. Territories differ but the number of churches is somewhere between fifty-five and seventy. Some parts of The Methodist Church have smaller districts, but out west we tend to have more congregations in our districts.

Somebody once called the district superintendent the business end of the episcopacy. Certainly he is the man who is closest to the local churches and ministers. He is the man both ministers and laymen turn to in case of trouble. At one time, he held four Quarterly Conferences in each local church but today that has been reduced to two, and sometimes to one. He is closer to being a pastor to the pastors than any other man, and he has a more objective view of each local congregation than any other man. This office was established in 1792 and has become such an integral part of our system that it would be unthinkable to tamper with it seriously unless Methodists decided to wreck their polity.

My first Cabinets were inherited, of course, and they had more to teach me than I could learn easily. Always I remember their patience with thanksgiving; and without exception, I had their complete loyalty. In a little while it seemed clear to me that the appointment of superintendents was one of the bishop's most important responsibilities. I learned soon enough their importance and their necessity. So far as the Methodist structure is concerned, the district superintendency is a cornerstone.

What kind of man makes a good superintendent? In a little while a series of principles began to stand out in my mind and every passing year has made them clearer. For one thing, he must be a successful pastor. There have been times when a bishop solved a problem by putting a man on his cabinet because he did not know where else to put him. This is always a mistake because the brethren are not so stupid as we sometimes wish they were and they see the picture clearly. All we succeed in doing through this procedure is to lower the office in the eyes of the conference and cheapen it in the eyes of the ministry. I will not appoint a superintendent who does not have a good record as a pastor. He may not be the best-liked man in the conference, but he must be respected. The job is not always done by the fellow who can win popularity contests, although his personal relations must be considerably above the average. The Methodist Church holds the bishop accountable for the area program and he must appoint superintendents who are not merely well-meaning men with no aggressive spirit. Churches need and want leadership, and even if a man is a driver, he will win support if he is fair and committed to the large tasks.

Superintendents must be men with wide enough vision to see beyond their own districts. Each one fights for the best leadership he can get for his own churches, but now and again he must surrender a strong man for an important job in another place. He strengthens the conference by strengthening his own district, but he must not strengthen his district at the expense of the conference. So, when we have talked it all through, I expect each man to accept the decision as if it were his own and stand behind it as if he had made it himself. No one is to go out of a cabinet meeting and say that he was outvoted. This happened in only one instance that I know about, and it did not happen again.

The district superintendent will have a great influence for good or ill on young preachers. He must be the kind of man they turn to easily and they must have confidence in his judgment. I have known men who became embittered because of some early experience with a superintendent. If possible, I want men who can get our young preachers off to the right start. Sometimes this kind of man is not immediately apparent, but he develops the gift. One of the best men I ever knew in this respect did his work so unobtrusively that his outstanding record with young preachers did not show until his term was practically finished.

My idea of administration is to find good men and give them freedom. District superintendents deal with such intricate affairs as finding the right locations for new churches, guiding preachers through difficult personal crises, keeping the pressure on lazy men and churches, helping official boards to get a vision of the world and the church. They have more authority and more responsibility than bishops in some other communions. Besides all this, I want them to be good preachers and able to inspire good preaching both by precept and example.

They need to be men of judgment. A wrong or hasty decision can upset the whole program and destroy the morale of a district and a conference. They need to communicate well, which is far from easy. One of the most democratic men I ever knew was always in hot water because laymen and ministers thought he was dictatorial. It was the way he put things, and apparently nothing could be done about it. He needed the gift of the man who said he always let them have his way. The fellow who should never be a superintendent is the man who loses his temper or writes letters in anger. Such men can serve God in some places, but not on the Cabinet of an Annual Conference.

Now some people are of the opinion that in a Cabinet political considerations play a large part. I have never found it so. I have never known of a superintendent trying to place a man because of his theological school or because his father was important in the conference. Close friendships always play some part, I suppose, but my superintendents have always preferred the stranger they thought could do the job over the friend they knew could not do it. Actually the only question we ever consider seriously is whether the man is the best man available to put in this place. I wish that every young Methodist preacher would get this idea in his head right at the beginning. I wish that every theological seminary would teach that there is no trick to it at all. No special wire-pulling or political maneuvering will succeed. It is the record, boys, just the record.

Every Methodist preacher has a friend at court. No matter how strained a relation may have become, every superintendent is out to fight for the best deal he can make for his own men. This is just standard procedure and may not be altogether altruistic, but men who have to give and take with one another soon develop the habit of doing their best for the men on their district. I would rather trust my future to a Methodist Cabinet than to any man or group of men in the world. I would feel certain that I would receive the best place available—and probably more than I deserved.

Some districts, because of their constituent churches, are stronger than others. A growing suburb is bound to have more to report than the inner city. One cannot measure the effectiveness of a district by statistics alone, any more than one can measure a church in that manner. The superintendent who can keep morale high and develop a spirit of unity and co-operation is earning his salary. In one instance, I know that men did difficult and almost impossible things so that they would not disappoint their superintendent or let their brethren down. I have had several superintendents who stood ready to help any man with a particularly difficult financial problem in his church. It was not a surprise when these men reported their missionary and benevolence giving 100 per cent of their apportionment.

More and more it has become clear to me that the Methodist polity demands that its programs be channeled through the district superintendents and set up on a district basis. This is the secret of getting every church involved in the program. I do not mean to minimize the importance of board secretaries, for these men too are key figures. But the superintendent has a relationship with his men that no other person can have. In the Southern California-Arizona Conference we have adopted the pattern of having the whole Cabinet in on the planning of all our enterprises. We make a superintendent the chairman of our main undertakings and we have adopted the idea that the Cabinet is the executive part of our organization. Whenever a conference program tries to bypass the Cabinet, it has a fifth wheel on the vehicle and is destined to travel a slow and rough road.

When all the district superintendents of The Methodist Church meet for their quadrennial gathering, it is a great meeting. Here are men who cover every square foot of American soil and deal with the churches at country crossroads, in hamlets, and in metropolitan areas. They are not theoretical experts who float around dealing with theories, but leaders face to face with laymen and preachers in churches ranging from twenty to eight thousand members. They know the church at its best and at its worst, and no other man in Methodism knows it better. I wish that every Methodist preacher could have the opportunity of serving on a Cabinet at least once in his ministry. It would make him a better minister.

The president of a theological seminary where I was lecturing said to me one time, "If I had my way, I would make every theological professor leave the classroom every seven years and serve a church." I answered that the idea had merit and would be good for the professor and the theological seminary, but I did not think the church could stand it. Every district superintendent serves six years and then must serve a church for at least three years before he can be reappointed to a district. Like all rules, this one sometimes works a hardship, but the idea of superintendents having actual experience in local churches is good.

I must say a word about the fellowship of the Cabinet. Here is the bishop's family and here are the men he knows best and most intimately. They are together in all kinds of situations and they come to see each other under the most testing circumstances. A few times a year the wives are included in our meetings, for in the ministry they are as important as their husbands. A bishop can pay no minister a higher compliment than to ask him to serve on the Cabinet. Along with my membership in the Council of Bishops, I value my relationships with my Cabinet. It makes up for the emptiness a fellow feels in being removed from the ministry of a church.

□ □ □

TELEVISION   The measure of a civilization is not so much its techniques as its purposes. It is not how clever it is but how good. Does it have some sense of the worth of persons, and is it dedicated to the increase of moral capacity and the enlargement of personal opportunities? To what end is its progress in science pointed? Usually there is some particular activity which reveals its hidden aims and gives the essential clue to the condition of its spiritual and moral life. In our case I think that clue is television.

I doubt that there is anything in our life today that reveals more completely the cheapness, the vulgarity, the tawdriness, and the stupidity of our society than do television commercials. This applies both to their quantity and to their quality. It was a sad thing that our first use of atomic fission was a bomb. It is also a sad thing that the miracle of television was turned over to the hucksters, who have never been noted for their taste. This modern wonder of entertainment and education has been surrendered to the pitchmen trying to make a fast sale for their employers, and almost without any resistance.

To look at American television would give the impression that all Americans do is brush their teeth, drink beer, smoke cigarettes, buy soap to make them dainty, put on deodorants to keep them smelling nice, and feed their dogs and cats better food than half the world can feed its children. And for these high aims, drama, music, or any product of the artist's brain and hand are to be used. The end is always a sale. The world must think we have become a nation of morons at the excitement shown by beautiful women and handsome men over such inconsequential things. What would they do to register concern if something important were offered them?

The whole thing is based on the premise that sincerity is convincing. Not anymore. The fellow holding up a package of cigarettes talks with the unction of an old-time evangelist pleading for another sinner to hit the sawdust trail. The mother crying out in anguish because Johnny forgot to brush his teeth puts on the same expression you would expect if she had just discovered he had sold his soul to the devil. The frantic car salesman is offering you salvation and the finance company wants to give you money. Religion has entered the home—only it is phony religion which has substituted easy payments and trinkets for grace and power. There is a story about a child objecting to the sermon in the church service because the "commercial was too long." I wonder if our children are being surfeited with false values and mere professional sincerity so that they will lose their ability to recognize the real things when they meet them.

Some of the commercials are fine. They have a clever twist which amuses and soothes. The lively jingles, the cartoon characters who satirize people—indeed, any approach that does not take itself too seriously—are bearable. I do not object to a company's getting its product mentioned if it is paying for the program. But trying to make the purchase of a tube of shaving cream or a mouth wash a big, crucial event determining human destiny is enough to make a sane man physically, emotionally, spiritually sick.

We talk a good deal today about what is wrong with us. Preachers always take off on this tack somewhere in the sermon, and editorial writers in newspapers and magazines have little trouble in finding things to view with alarm. Not many, however, are willing to say that a lot of this trouble is inevitable within the framework of our Madison Avenue psychology. Decent living is a bit more than finding enough money to buy things. Yet from morning until night we are bombarded with buying pressures from papers, billboards, radios, and television sets. One of my young preachers told me that his wife saw so much advertised on TV she thought she must have that it almost broke up their marriage. What about the wife who has never heard that there is anything more in life than new styles and gadgets?

I do not want to give the impression that cultural and educational programs are all I want. Not at all. We could stand a good deal more than we get, but evening after evening of improving our minds would be too much for me. If I want to improve my mind, I read a book. Television is for relaxation so far as I am concerned, and I have amazingly little curiosity as to what some celebrity thinks about the world situation. A lively discussion of a controversial subject is often interesting, but for every good one there are a dozen such programs that are academic, dull, and too long. A good mystery or a baseball game will get my vote every time.

I like westerns. There is something so far-fetched, unreal, and reactionary about them that they please me. Here are the good old days when men lived in the open with no office routine and no income tax. There was no desperate pursuit of a few more dollars to pay back the finance company. If your ranch was going to be taken from you, it was because of a villain you could fight with the help of a brave sheriff or a noble gunslinger. Shucks, even trouble was romantic and never monotonous.

How fine it must have been to have everything either black or white with no problem of deciding between two almost imperceptibly different shades of gray. What a relief to know that evil can be destroyed with a six-shooter. How hopeful to know that one good man can lick ten bad ones. This is the world of make-believe and the Land of Oz for weary adults. There is even something rather comforting about the clichés and the threadbare plots. None of this surprise stuff in westerns, and the fellow who tries to give a story a strange twist at the end is a betrayer of an established art form. All of this talk about "adult westerns" makes me laugh. Their appeal is to boys and not men, but as the psychologists like to remind us, childhood is a perpetual hangover for nearly all men.

Television is constantly being urged to raise the quality of its programs. But if you are going to turn out quantity you cannot have quality. How ridiculous to think that you can broadcast from 6 A.M. until 1 A.M. seven days a week and have a high standard of excellence. You are doomed to have 90 per cent of it moronic and bearable only for those who are afraid of silence and prefer to hear voices speaking drivel. Personally I would like to see a station schedule about four hours a day and appeal to certain tastes. After all, radio stations now have become music stations or news stations. Specialization is taking place everywhere else—even in the church—why not in television? Certainly we do not need so many stations broadcasting the same tripe at the same time.

I do not want government control for several reasons. For one thing, we have too much of it already in too many fields. I do not believe this comes about because government is aggressive, but because society is lethargic. Somebody has to fill the vacuum, and the same people who stand up and cheer for free enterprise are the first to demand government assistance for their own affairs. But state programs are inevitable propaganda. Some politician wants to enlighten the people or give them what he thinks is good for them. Television in Russia seemed like pretty dull stuff to me, though admittedly I could not understand the language. But there was too much about how happy the children and youth were and too many tours through factories.

As long as there are unscrupulous exploiters abroad in the land, there must be some social controls. They should be kept as loose as possible and administered by a commission which is more of a clearing-house through which the public can make its desires known. Any control agency ought to see to it that the owners of stations are responsible, moral persons and that no one who can think in commercial terms only shall be allowed to operate a station. For this is something vastly more than a commercial enterprise; television is education, culture, propaganda, taste-setter, and definer of purposes and ideals. Minimum standards must be set, but we want as little censorship as possible. Only an authoritarian state or church which claims the right to decide all questions of morals and behavior for its members will insist that it must pass on what people are to see or read. It is not the American way and it is not the free-church way.

Thus far, the churches have not done very well as far as religious television is concerned. For myself, all I need to know is that a program is religious to make me stay as far away from it as possible. Ninety-nine times out of a hundred it will be corny, trite, with a moral as obvious as garlic. Often it will have a minister, a priest, or a rabbi whose well-meaning but stupid ways make any decent pagan rejoice in his religious prejudices. Sometimes our fumbling is due to lack of funds, but sometimes it is caused by not knowing how to make religion anything but frosting on the cake. Men who are seeking for the bread of life are not much impressed with such fluff.

I do not know if there is an answer to this problem. The religious racketeers with their phony healings and promises have no problem because they have no ethics. There are enough suckers to support them and they will continue to exploit this lucrative field as long as the FCC will wink its eye. I wonder how Christianity in America has survived under the barrage of so-called religious programs on the Sunday radio. Television is not quite so bad yet, but given time it may get that way. How does the church get its good news to the people via these mass communications media?

I would like to see a series of programs based on the Congregational heritage in New England, or the brave preachers of the Revolution, or the Methodist circuit riders moving west. There are any number of great men and women, both past and present, whose lives are full of drama and who loved God by serving men. What the Lutherans have done in the film Martin Luther indicates that the churches are not unable to produce some great pictures. But thus far, little seems to be happening in this field to make us shout.

In the meantime, the church must find some way to make its criticism of television effective. We have a duty to help the better and make the worse unprofitable. The Broadcasting and Film Commission of the National Council of Churches and the denominational commissions in this field could render a great service by spreading the word about good programs and warning us about poor ones. Rather than produce so much second-rate stuff ourselves, it would be fine if we could encourage the production of programs with sound moral foundations as well as high entertainment value. It is not necessary for the church to put its brand on every program that is to be regarded as religious. Sometimes commercial companies give artists more freedom than the church is willing to allow. We are often incapable of showing proper appreciation for the program with deep ethical and spiritual implications unless the program carries a religious label. More than one Hollywood producer has told me that Protestants sometimes feebly object but are silent when it comes to commendation.

But the Christian church ought to counteract the television gospel that human problems have physical solutions. We surround our children with this propaganda and wonder why it is they so often put spiritual affairs in the same category with fairy tales. We have to free ourselves from the complete domination of television by commercial interests. The answer may be in pay television or in more educational channels. But the continued dominance of our life by advertising cannot help but warp our sense of values and make us assume that the final goal of living is selling. I do not want an emasculated entertainment that is all stuffy virtue; but I would like to have it possible for a family to hear some music or watch a play without fifteen salesmen rudely interrupting Beethoven or Shakespeare.

LOS ANGELES   In 1952 I was assigned to the Los Angeles Area of The Methodist Church. It included Southern California, the southern tip of Nevada, Arizona, and the Hawaiian Islands. At that time it consisted of three conferences—the Southern California-Arizona Conference, the Hawaii Mission Conference, and the Latin American Provisional Conference. Since then the Latin American Conference has been merged with the Anglo conferences.

The polity of The Methodist Church assigns a bishop to one area for four years, after which he comes up for appointment the same as any Methodist preacher. I knew that Bishop James C. Baker was retiring in 1952, but I had no expectation of being his successor. As a matter of fact, it was not until fifteen minutes before the bishops' appointments were read that I learned I was to be sent to Los Angeles. For while there had been rumors aplenty, I have long learned to discount all of them by at least 80 per cent and most of them by 100 per cent.

It was a radical change from Portland. The country was different, the spirit was different, and the responsibilities were so big they scared me. The offices were on Sunset Boulevard just across from the old Plaza and next to Olvera Street. One morning my secretary placed

117

on my desk the list of requests for my presence at dedication services of new churches, my appointments for the next two days, and the meetings I must attend that week. When I went out to lunch, the smog was thick and stung my eyes. I had the desperate feeling of being trapped on an assembly line and longed for the openness of the Northwest. My old friend Roy Smith telephoned me and I deluged him with my self-pity and despair. He listened and then began to talk about the future of the Southwest with its challenges and its opportunities. He made me feel so much better that I agreed to stay until the end of the week.

That was the only low moment and from that time on it has been with a sense of great privilege that I have done my work in this section of the church. Enough has been written about the growth and expansion of Southern California so that I will not bother to put down the figures, the percentages, the prophecies of future population, etc. It is enough to say that one of the main problems of the churches is to keep up with the expanding communities. Sometimes when I'm caught in the freeway traffic—and that is about every day—it seems to me that only a fool would live in such crowds unless he had to. But I have to and in my more objective moments, I know that this Los Angeles Area is where I want to be more than any place in the world.

One of my chief delights has been my dealings with laymen. It is not easy for a bishop to know his laymen, for unlike the minister he is not in regular contact with them. I was helped by a luncheon which was given for me in 1952 at the new Statler Hotel. To everybody's surprise more than a thousand men came out—to see the new hotel, no doubt, as one of my friends put it. That affair has become a tradition and those luncheons now take place in other cities in the area. We have some great laymen, as do all churches, and by coming to know them a large part of my frustration and loneliness has been dissipated.

Our attitude toward theology and the church is always affected deeply by our circumstances. Continental theology is different from American theology because European Christians have been through things we have never experienced. Theology must differ from age to age and from place to place. This is not because it has no central integrity, but because it is wide as life and every human condition brings Christianity into fresh focus. Each human condition illuminates afresh an affirmation of our faith. So we should appreciate our differences and learn from them without feeling a compulsion to eliminate them.

The same principle holds for church life. Believe me, The Methodist Church is not in California what it is in New England. And it is still different in the Middle West and in the South. The minister in Connecticut may find himself fighting to hold his own, while the same man in California would be fighting to keep up with the procession. This is bound to affect each man's attitude toward his task. It will also affect his theology.

I have seen this around the world and it is observable in history. There was, from the beginning, the Hebrew emphasis and the Greek influence. The church behind the Iron Curtain is one thing and the church in England is another. What the Christian church has had to do through the centuries is determine the central core of the gospel and never let that be compromised. It has rightly labeled any attempt to tamper with the essentials as heresy. But it has had to have wisdom enough to see that the Christian truth has to pass through the webs of racial cultures and geographical differences. That it has been able to do this is a sign of God's presence in it, and indeed, it is hardly less than a miracle.

I was at Colgate-Rochester Seminary some time ago, and in one of the discussion periods after my lecture, the question of federated churches came up. I expressed my candid opinion that they are one of the poorest arrangements and, so far as I could see, almost a complete loss. They are neither fish nor fowl and become so parochial that they lose any vision of the world. Over my dead body, I said, would any more such monstrosities be formed in my area. The man who raised the question was incensed. He told about churches in little villages in upper New York which had to federate to endure. This, he insisted, was saving the church. Maybe! But I still think that only a desperate situation can justify them, and wherever the church is on the march they will not be tolerated. There are better ways than federation to witness to ecumenicity.

One of my greatest thrills has been to be a part of the creation of new churches. Although we built sixty new churches in ten years, we were still behind what we should have done. I found that my outstanding young men would gladly accept appointments to three or five acres of bare land. We helped them financially, but the chief burden was on them. They called in the neighborhoods and rounded up the charter members. They met with building committees and planned the first units. They worshiped in schoolhouses, lodge halls, dance studios, until they had their first building. And then some of them tithed their budgets and building campaigns to help start other churches.

Young families came into these new congregations. Often, having drifted from the church, their children brought them back and they became active and enthusiastic. Anyone who thinks the church has lost its appeal or its evangelistic passion ought to visit the new congregations in the Southwest.

Not many of these people had any experience in running a church. They were put on boards and committees and then began to tackle their jobs with all kinds of new ideas. This was not always clear profit, and some of their methods horrified the old-timers who had never seen it after this fashion. But the young preachers all agreed that it was fine to have a church where you never heard, "We never did it this way," or "We tried this once and it did not work." In this expanding situation there is the sharp cutting edge of people uncaptured by the past and unbound by tradition. They have the radical idea that when you join a church, you must go to work.

Bishop Baker told me one time long ago that he had never seen a conference where there was such unity of action as in this one. I have found it so and it has been a joy to be bishop in such an environment. That does not mean that the boys always agree or that they are sheep. Far from it! Our programs are debated up and down the districts before we arrive at the actual session of the conference. But once the program is voted, we go together without further holding back. I do not imply that we are unique, but only that we bear witness to the genius of the Methodist polity when it is understood and practiced.

There is no more varied or marvelous scenery than in this area. Arizona with its Grand Canyon and its beautiful deserts; Hawaii, which has been called rightly "the paradise of the Pacific"; California with its mountains and seashore—all constitute an affirmation that God loves beauty. The people do not always measure up to the scenery. Las Vegas lives on gambling which, in spite of the glamour of The Strip, is always cheap and sordid. Hollywood has more than its share of scandalous behavior from movie stars who practice a serial type of bigamy. We experience reactionary pressures and are confronted by our share of medieval thinking. But there is no place where I have ever been that is more alive and exciting.

You would find, for example, that the vast majority of Hollywood stars are decent, hard-working, religious people. You would find also that Las Vegas has some of the finest laymen in the church. There is an astounding growth in cultural life with an amazing number of writers and artists making their homes in this area. Los Angeles is becoming something vastly more than a place of weird religions, retired fanatics, and tasteless publicity stunts. It is one of the centers of art and literature, and it attracts those who desire enlightenment of the mind and spirit, as well as those seeking beaches, mountains, and sunshine.

I sometimes wonder what will come out of this land of sun worshipers and outdoor addicts in the long years ahead. J. B. Priestley, the English writer, took a rather dim view of the Southwest when he wrote about it some years ago in *Midnight on the Desert*. To him it seemed so impermanent, and he viewed Los Angeles as a kind of deluxe camping. But with the population moving west and the center of national power shifting toward the setting sun, it looks pretty permanent to me. For better or worse, it is bound to have an increasing influence on the quality of our American civilization. Whenever I stop for a moment to catch my breath, I find myself saying with the psalmist: "The lines have fallen for me in pleasant places."

We built our own home in the Hollywood Hills, which are really the Santa Monica Mountains. For the first time in our lives my wife and I owned some property, and believe me it does affect you. There is something to this doctrine of the value of private ownership, and I have come to believe that it is one of the foundations of democracy. I found myself working in the yard and enjoying it, which never happened to me when we lived in parsonages. My whole attitude

121

toward my city became more personal, more concerned. I became aware of taxes; and maybe it is a weakness that preachers, priests, and rabbis often make their pronouncements with no sense of it costing them anything financially. Anyway, communal ownership strikes me as one of the hardest blows against the dignity of the individual, and I think that God meant each man to have the right to sit under his own vine and fig tree.

From our hilltop we can see Catalina Island on a clear day—which is not every day. At night the vast panorama of Los Angeles stretches out before us with its acres of lights. In the summer the gentle, cooling breezes from the Pacific keep us cool. In the winter we have yet to see the temperature fall below 38 degrees. If I go east, there is Arizona, a winter playground. If I go west, there is Hawaii, a playground all the year around. I sat next to the governor of California at a luncheon one day and he asked me how I enjoyed my work. I replied to him that I was drawing a salary from The Methodist Church for doing what I would gladly pay The Methodist Church for the opportunity of doing, if I could afford it. Which I cannot. And it is perhaps wise to stop right here!

I PROCLAIM
WITHOUT FEAR...

MISSIONARIES   When I was a boy, my mother sometimes entertained the Foreign Missionary Society. They studied some book, planned to collect some clothes or raise a little money, and drank tea. The whole affair seemed typically adult and useless to me and the occasional appearance of returned missionaries, with a few notable exceptions, did nothing to change my mind. I am still unable to understand why missionaries return and preach sermons instead of telling home congregations about their work and their experiences. I suppose that it is because a chance to preach before a fair-sized congregation is a temptation not to be denied. But what people want to hear is an account of life in the Congo or what the gospel has been able to accomplish in Nepal.

I am ashamed to say that for the first twenty years of my ministry I took missionary offerings and used missionary illustrations without any real comprehension of what this mighty enterprise was doing. I had some conviction that Christianity had to be missionary-minded, but I had only a foggy idea of the part the missionary played in a non-Christian society. Since this is probably true of most ministers and laymen, I am surprised that we do as well as we do in supporting the worldwide mission of the church. Actually we have little more enthusiasm than the average citizen has for the Community Chest, and we give missions the same niggardly support.

The General Conference of 1948 approved a plan whereby the bishops, once every quadrennium, would visit a mission area of The Methodist Church. I chose Japan, since the Portland Area had adopted it as its main interest abroad. After attending the World Methodist Conference in Oxford in 1951, my wife and I went to Israel and then we made our way eastward to Singapore, the Philippines, and, finally, Japan. It was an unforgettable experience, and one that made me wish every layman and every minister could see the gospel at work in a non-Christian culture.

The mission schools of Malaya impressed me greatly. After my return home, I heard a British government official at Rotary say that education in Malaya had been stimulated and lifted by the schools of The Methodist Church. I was greatly impressed by the vitality of Protestantism in the Philippines, and particularly in Manila. It seemed to me that a small minority would be on the defensive and somewhat hesitant in its witness. I did not find it so. One afternoon I spoke to the Protestant group on the campus of the university. There was an almost electric quality of devotion in the air. Those students had paid a price for their faith, since most of them came from Catholic homes where they were under family pressures to remain Catholics. Protestants had influence far beyond their numbers and they had a gallantry and joy in their religion that was not generally observable back home.

On arrival in Tokyo we were taken under the wings of Dr. and Mrs. Floyd Shacklock. They knew the country, the language, and had had long experience both with missions and with the Japanese people. In the next month we covered the country, going from north to south and visiting what seemed like hundreds of churches and institutions. Being new at the job, it seemed to us that we must see everything; and if anyone thinks such a trip is a vacation, he will change his mind after just one day. These episcopal visits are about the hardest work I do, and they were never set up to give a bishop a vacation. But they are inspiring experiences, and I do not know any other men who have such opportunities to get into the heart of another culture so quickly. For missionaries know more about what the people are thinking and the actual conditions than most diplomats and businessmen.

We took off one day on a long train trip to the north. There, after crossing over to Hokkaido, the northernmost island, I spent a few days with the ministers and laymen of the Kyodan (the united church of Japan) in Hakodate. Methodism joined the Kyodan, and our missionary work has been done within its framework. I sat in churches without heat and caught a new vision of the church at work at its primary task—evangelism. We came back south and stopped at Hirosaki where they raise some of the largest and most beautiful apples in the world. Each apple, while still on the tree, was wrapped in paper to protect it from birds.

Besides the great schools and colleges, I saw the church at work in social settlements like Aikei Gakuen in Tokyo and in rural centers in Tsuyazaki and Fukuoka in Kyushu, the southernmost island. Believe me, we may still argue about the social gospel versus the personal gospel at home, but there is no argument of the subject in the mission field. It is perfectly obvious to the missionaries that the gospel is both a proclamation and a demonstration, and everything that has to do with human welfare is of interest to the Christian church. I take considerable satisfaction in observing that our Christian social concern has forced other religions to show more interest in the physical welfare of people. It should not be of primary importance that someone else gets some credit if the job is done.

I went to the Island of Shikoku over one weekend. A young missionary and his wife and small children were doing an outstanding job in shepherding congregations and extending the Christian work. I remember that the three-year-old boy had picked up enough Japanese so that he could act as interpreter for his parents in some instances. There I was initiated into the Japanese tea ceremony and experienced the beauty of Japanese country life. I preached one morning at the newest church, which was meeting in the home of its wealthiest member, a retired army colonel. After the service, the congregation came out into the street and sang "God Be with You Till We Meet Again." I have never forgotten that little group of Christians, perhaps thirty in number, waving us on our way with that old hymn ringing in my ears.

I do not know a more beautiful land than Japan. Who can ever forget Nikko with its giant redwoods, its temples, and its appearance of heavenly charm? Kyoto, with its temples and gardens, and Nara are cities unique in their beauty. The Japanese were so courteous. And when the train pulled away from a station, a platform of people bowing their good-byes gave the feeling of royalty departing. I was back in Tokyo six years later and saw great changes. Most of the dress was Western and there was much less polite bowing. Now it was a Western city including traffic, hurry, and rudeness. What a price we pay for what we call progress!

We were riding with a young missionary to Nara and lost our way. The young man asked a policeman directions, and he told me what the man had said. In response to the question "Is this the way to Nara?" the policeman had answered, "Yes, but turn left at the next corner, then left again. Go three blocks, turn left and then right." Which was to say bluntly, "Turn around and go back in the opposite direction." But no Japanese would be so blunt, and so the policeman began by making us feel we were practically on the road, although we were going farther from Nara with every mile.

I visited Hiroshima, where we have a high school and college for girls. It seemed to me there would be obvious hatred for Americans who had dropped the first atomic bomb. There was no such indication, and even the girls who had been horribly scarred by the explosion greeted us with gentle kindness. I sat one moonlit night on the porch of the Kwassui Girls High School and Junior College in Nagasaki and listened to a woman describe the horror of the second atomic explosion in that city. There was almost a kind of pride at having been through the worst and a quiet dedication to the cause of peace that had a fierce intensity about it. The whole new spirit seemed symbolized to me in the creation of the International Christian University in Tokyo. Ah, those were the days when the reconciliation of enemies and the establishment of peace seemed not altogether impossible.

The picture which the average church member has of missionaries is so false it is pitiful. For many people the missionary is an elderly, plain, unmarried woman dressed in black who will pray for you publicly at the drop of a hat. Her male counterpart is thought of as a dull, excessively pious brother who would rather be caught dead than laughing. I do not know if that picture ever had any reality, but I know it has none now.

In my judgment, the church is at its best in its missionary personnel. I have seen middle-aged and elderly women who, for sheer courage and sparkle, beat anything you will find in the most fashionable churches of the United States. I know young couples who, for attractiveness and ability, can take their places in any profession in any city in the world. Whenever I make a missionary visit, I take new courage because of the kind of young people who are giving their lives to this cause. There must be some who do not measure up—as there are in all professions. But the general picture is so good I am tempted to covet these wonderful young people for my own area. And this is not just true of Japan, for I have observed the same high quality in South America, in Africa, in India, in Europe, and, indeed, around the whole wide world. One of my laymen said to me after a visit to a mission field, "Business would pay twenty thousand a year to get the kind of representatives abroad that the church gets for one fourth that amount."

These people can do things. They know how to build buildings and repair cars. They are as capable at repairing their homes as if they had specialized in plumbing and carpentry at college. They cannot call the corner garage or service station, and for resourcefulness and self-sufficiency they are unexcelled. And those wonderful young wives who bring their babies into the world miles from what we would call civilization and raise their children in strange places and lonely villages! The days of courage and the spirit of the frontier are not ended yet, and if the American church could just understand this, it would strengthen its weakness and deepen its spiritual shallowness.

During the Second World War, many a GI found missionaries in places where he never suspected any white person would be. Because they were there, he found friends when it was a matter of life and death for him. After the war we found there was a reservoir of good will for America which, to a large extent, was the creation of the missionary enterprise of the churches. These people knew more about what the people were thinking than the CIA. Here was the only considerable body of men and women who had gone abroad to give and not to get. Now comes the belated Peace Corps, which is a governmental attempt to do what the church has been doing for years. May God give it success; but as Frank Laubach said to me one time, "Only the church can save the world, for only the church has what the world must have to be saved." If you want to see the church at its best, visit a mission field.

One of my ministerial friends has a son who decided to enter the ministry. He married just before going to theological seminary, and his bride asked her mother-in-law what courses she should take to prepare herself to be a minister's wife. The young lady was shocked when her husband's mother replied: "I would take a course in plumbing." She went on to say that her husband would be away much of the time and even when he was home, he would be so involved in other matters that household repairs would wait weeks for attention. I have thought of this when on the mission field and observed how missionaries and their wives learn how to do everything from repairing a leaky roof to replacing a leaky pipe in the basement. No ivory towers for them!

As I look back over what I have written about missions, it sounds somewhat overly exuberant and a little juvenile in its enthusiasm. But I shall let it stand, for this is the way I felt after my first visit to a missionary field. And while enthusiasm often needs to be tempered by criticism, still I feel my heart strangely warmed whenever missions are mentioned. Thank God for the people who leave their homes and their people to preach and teach Christ by precept and example in faraway places with strange-sounding names.

SEMINAR   In the summer of 1950, I decided rather suddenly to go to Europe with Sherwood Eddy and the American Seminar. There were about fifty in the party, and it was one of the most rewarding summers of my life. It was worth a year of college and I wonder if the hundreds of alumni of this seminar also look back upon it as a high point in their experiences. It was said that this would be Dr. Eddy's last trip, which was a slight exaggeration. He was seventy-nine years old then, but he is still going strong and he accompanied several seminars after 1950. I remember he showed me some Scotch tweed he had purchased in London and said, "Bishop, I will be wearing this for ten years." You do not think of Sherwood Eddy as an old man and you never will.

We crossed on the "Queen Mary" and had lectures each day on the voyage. My most embarrassing moment was trying to stay awake one day after taking a dramamine tablet because the sea was rough. Too late I learned that these things simply put me to sleep. The company was mostly preachers, teachers, social workers. There were a few stuffed shirts, but on the whole it was a stimulating group bent on learning and observing as well as enjoying. A somber note was struck when the radio reported the outbreak of the Korean War while we were at sea. This inspired a most interesting lecture by Dr. Eddy on Syngman Rhee who had been his longtime friend. He showed us the New Testament Rhee had read which had converted him to Christianity while in prison awaiting execution. I remembered all of that when I met Dr. Rhee some years later and I remembered it again when he was exiled and repudiated by his country in 1960.

After our arrival in London, we settled down for about a week of lectures at Toynbee Hall. Through his long experience, Dr. Eddy could arrange to have national and educational leaders speak to his seminars so that we heard a long list of authorities and famous men. Dr. James Mallon was the perfect host and Toynbee Hall, of which he had been the head for some time, was one of the great pioneer social settlements in England.

Mallon was a great admirer of Churchill and gave us some of his personal observations of one of the great men of the twentieth century. He told us that people flocked to his meetings when he was running for office because they knew that something unusual would emerge. Whenever Churchill was in a situation, Churchill was always three fourths of it. He was at his best in the rough give-and-take and heckling of British political meetings. A man shouted out in response to one of Churchill's arguments, "Rot!" The speaker replied that "my friend is no doubt expressing what is in his mind."

In one of Churchill's speeches before the war, he had referred to fascism and communism as despotisms of the left and right, and ultimately the same thing. A voice from the balcony called out, "Oh, they're poles apart—poles apart." Churchill paused for a moment and said, "Poles apart? Well, consider these poles. At one pole you will find penguins but not at the other. There are, no doubt, other differences. But at both poles you will find the same freezing temperature, the same barren landscapes where nothing can grow, and where life becomes bitter and hopeless."

131

Churchill, said Mallon, had the gift for the inevitable words. He was no reactionary but had a vision of the whole situation and was a champion of all the people. There was an exciting quality about him so that even the charwomen worked harder in his building. He could cut down his opponents with sharp words. He said of Sir Stafford Cripps, "There but for the grace of God, goes God." Later on he referred to Attlee as "a sheep in sheep's clothing," which was unfair according to Dean Acheson. Mallon felt, and I share that same conviction, that Sir Winston Churchill was the man of the hour from 1939 to 1945.

We heard of the beginnings of Toynbee Hall in 1884, when Samuel Barnett, pastor of a fashionable West End church, came down into the East End to serve St. Jude's in the slums. He enlisted young men from Oxford and Cambridge to give their time to teach and serve under the conviction that education was a trust and a responsibility. It was one of the first great experiments in adult education, and teaching was still one of its main activities. The foundation of Barnett's philosophy was that nothing much could be done from afar, so the university students lived in the neighborhood, as did the Barnett family. This kind of service is something quite different from the man who prayed: "O Lord, use me—especially in an advisory capacity." The Toynbee idea was the way of the Incarnation, and it is the only way that accomplishes much lasting good.

We had a number of professors from the University of London analyze the European situation and give statistics regarding production, unemployment, education, and food. I was impressed with the easy, objective way these men regarded communism as compared with the American hysteria. They seemed bent on protecting civil rights and letting "the blighters talk."

The blitz was fresh in the English minds and they told of the weird and pathetic happenings of that time of terror. Mallon said that one old lady at Toynbee went down to the shelter at the first warning and did not come up for three days. A man in the country had agreed to take nine elderly people and was somewhat nonplussed when they sent him nineteen expectant mothers. One night in the blackness of the shelter, Mallon overheard this conversation: "Joe, they are taking me to the hospital and I may die. If I live I shall be ugly. Could you still put up with me, Joe?"And Joe allowed as how he could. Whenever I get annoyed with some trait in the English national character, I remember some of this sheer courage and thank God to be a part of that heritage.

Lady Astor spoke about some of the slightly scandalous reports of her activities in the papers. "Oh, well," she said, "I had a bad press. But then, the press is always wrong, isn't it?" She remarked that she took a very dim view of most modern psychological theories. A person, she insisted, is always frustrated when he does wrong, and that's that. All the talk about Abraham Lincoln as a testimony to the greatness of the common man sickened her. He was not so common, she commented, seeing there has never been another one like him.

Creech-Jones, former Secretary of Colonies, spoke about England's colonial problems, and Herbert Morrison discussed the Labor Party's accomplishments and hopes. Lord Halifax criticized the Labor policies and told what the Conservatives would change if they came into power. I had the impression that like the conservatives in the United States, they were trying desperately to find issues without upsetting the program which obviously had public support. They would lessen control here and there, but they would not tamper with the railroads or with public health. Both conservatives and liberals seemed to be facing a difficult national situation with calm realism. There was a remarkable lack of vituperation and no sign of hysteria. They may have passed through their "finest hour," but there was still greatness to be seen in the midst of austerity and sacrifice.

One of the best lectures was given by Harold Nicolson on the British monarchy and, for the first time, I began to have an appreciation for the royal court. The king, said the lecturer, has little power but much influence. He stands above party and is the symbol of the nation. I remember he said that England could never have a Hitler because "the king would not stand for it." Along with the Archbishop of Canterbury, the King of England symbolizes the history, destiny, and spirit of Great Britain.

We had a pleasant tea at Lambeth Palace with the Archbishop of Canterbury as our host. Dr. Geoffrey Fisher was a plain man with no pretenses or stuffiness, and we all liked him immensely. When he learned I was one of Bishop G. Bromley Oxnam's colleagues, he took

133

me into a corner and gave me five minutes alone. A little later, we had an hour with the so-called Red Dean of Canterbury. He seemed like an idealistic, almost otherworldly figure when it came to discussing the issues. Sherwood Eddy tried to drive him into a corner, but the old man gently slipped outside our attacks. As Dr. Eddy said earlier, some think he is one of God's fools, and some think he is just a plain damn fool. But he was never the victim of the scurrilous attacks that our statesmen and leaders, with much less reason, were subjected to under the McCarthy regime. They never had said even one good word for the Communists—which the Dean of Canterbury did quite often.

Arnold Toynbee was with us for an hour and the memory of that interview is still fresh in my mind. He had such a long perspective that it seemed to me that nothing in the morning papers could be very important. For the historian was thinking in terms of centuries and generations, while our minds were filled with the latest headlines and crises. To hear a man like that analyze the historical trends was like listening to God. He saw the stormy relations between East and West as productive of great new achievements in the future. For him, the religious issues were the real ones and the saint was more important than the politician. He reminded us that Magna Carta was born out of the period which produced England's worst king.

We had many more fine writers and political leaders address us in Holland, Switzerland, France, and Germany. Berlin was the most hated name during the war and five years later it was a symbol of freedom being threatened by the Communist tyranny. We change our enemies as easily as we change our coats, and those who would tell us that that there is inevitable conflict between certain peoples simply do not know their history. And neither do those who think a military victory wipes out the past.

One night in Frankfort, we were listening to a German intellectual who claimed that most Germans did not know what was happening to the Jews. They simply could not believe the rumors. We had been through Dachau the day before and the horror of that murder camp was upon us. Suddenly, the tour manager, himself a Jew, was on his feet. "The stench of Dachau filled the air for miles around," he said. "Don't tell me the Germans did not know what the Nazis were doing."

This man, who has been my dear friend for more than a decade, became the voice of Zola that night and his word was "J'accuse." I keep wondering what my role is when American subversive groups hold their meetings and preach their doctrines. I see a man pointing his finger at me and saying, "Of course you knew. What did you do?" For none of us are free from this poison, especially in a day when to scream loudly against the Communists excuses all sorts of denials of freedom. Our enemy, dear friends, is the fellow who, under some patriotic cover, attacks the democratic heritage of free discussion and the right to hold unpopular ideas.

PREACHING   I entered the Methodist ministry to preach. From the time when I was sixteen years old and made a speech (really a kind of sermon) in the student body assembly of my high school, I understood Paul's proclamation: "For if I preach the gospel, that gives me no ground for boasting. For necessity is laid upon me. Woe to me if I do not preach the gospel!" (I Cor. 9:16.) It is my conviction that anything less than this is not enough to be considered a call to preach. I meet too many young ministers who say in effect, "Well, I do not mind preaching. As a matter of fact, I rather enjoy it." This is not to say that such young men will not perform a valuable service for the church. But they will never be men with prophetic authority and pentecostal fire.

As a college student and then as a seminary student, I preached twice a week. Harry Emerson Fosdick was reported to have said that no man could prepare more than one sermon a week which would be worth hearing. I agree with him, and unless a man can be set free to do nothing but preach, one sermon a week is enough. So in those good old days, I leaned heavily on other men's sermons. Right from the beginning I admired simple language, clear outline, and a message relevant to my daily life.

I began by using notes but always I knew it would be better preaching if there were no notes. So, because preaching was my main ambition, I resolved to learn how to do it with freedom. From my seminary days onward, nothing went into my pulpit with me except my preparation and hard work. I have so few virtues that I mention (perhaps boast is the proper word) one quality which gives me great satisfaction. So far as I can recall, I have never stood in my pulpit without having prepared for the event to the very best of my ability. This is not to say that every sermon has seemed satisfactory to me. None of them have. But it has never been necessary to apologize to God or man because I let other things crowd into my time for preparation. I have neglected other matters connected with my work, but it never seemed permissible to give my congregation less than my best.

This was due largely to an ironbound schedule which became almost as much a part of me as breathing. I outlined my sermon on Wednesday morning and then talked it through Thursday, Friday, and Saturday mornings. Sunday morning I rarely got involved in other activities, although I broadcast over the radio before my service for several years. Sunday morning was my last chance to meditate on the sermon, although sometimes I am afraid it was merely worrying about it. But I could never be at ease if anything interfered with this schedule, and even when I was traveling, it was kept faithfully. Sometimes it meant getting up pretty early in the morning, but nothing went well unless I followed the routine.

I do not know what conscious aim other preachers have when they preach. For me it was to proclaim a conviction about God's nature, God's will, God's resources, God's promises. It was to bear a testimony to the truth of Christ and to help people see themselves as the objects of God's love revealed in Jesus. It was to create a faith that the gospel is the answer to all human questions and the solution to all human problems. It was to prophesy against evil and heal the brokenhearted. I would sometimes become so frustrated with my inadequacies that it seemed only a stupid egotist or a blind fool could continue as a preacher. But I have never been able to escape the conviction that preaching is nothing less than God in Christ using a poor, unworthy man to proclaim his Word.

It is the terrible vision of God and the horrible knowledge of one's own pettiness and sin that constitute the preacher's dilemma. One of my colleagues in the Council of Bishops once said that a preacher's wife has the impossible task of living with him all week and of regarding him as the voice of God on Sunday. For this and other reasons all preachers' wives are assured of heaven, for they have suffered enough hell on earth. But as long as the preacher himself does not succumb to pride, his situation is not to be envied either. Why should a congregation gather week after week to hear me? Do they not know how limited is my knowledge and how small is my virtue? I suppose this is the reason that the half hour from ten-thirty to eleven on Sunday mornings has always been agony of mind and spirit. Will anyone come today? Is my word worth even a moron's consideration? I tell you the man who is never nervous before he preaches and never suffers the despair of the damned when he finishes is either an angel or a fool.

Yet I would be less than candid not to confess that when the hour has struck and the text is announced, I come closest to understanding the psalmist's word about man: "Yet thou . . . dost crown him with glory and honor" (Ps. 8:5). For of all the privileges bestowed upon any of his creatures, to proclaim the unsearchable riches of Christ is surely the highest. Of all the tasks that men are given to do, preaching seems to me to be the greatest. You may recall that in *Moby Dick* Herman Melville speaks of the pulpit as the place where the storm is first described and where the fair breeze is first invoked. "Yes," he writes, "the world's a ship on its passage out, and not a voyage complete; and the pulpit is its prow."

While my present job does not involve preaching to a continuing congregation—which is a great personal loss—still I do as much or more preaching than when I was in the pastorate. And I have learned more about preachers than I knew then, for they have talked to me and so have their laymen. While I still have a very limited opportunity to hear other men preach, for what it is worth they seem to me to fail mostly at three points.

First, too many of us do not work on our preaching hard enough or long enough. The more gifted a man is, the more he is tempted to neglect his preparation. You listen to a man and he brings out an

137

interesting point here or there, but there is no sense of solid structure. He makes too much of one point and too little of another. He milks an illustration dry, and what would have been effective if kept short and sharp loses its cutting edge and gets wearisome. Such a man circles back to something already dealt with and there is no sense of the inevitable, forward march of the thought.

Secondly, too many preachers fail to organize their material so that it is at once plain and clear. The people leave with a vague sense of something religious having been said, but the points which give a subject distinctness are either hopelessly smudged and muddled or they were never there in the first place. I have lectured on this, written about it, and discussed it at every opportunity, but it has done little good. So many preachers will not believe that their first responsibility is to be understood. I still have church members come up after the sermon and say, with a kind of wonderment, "I understood you." To organize our material does not take special gifts and it does not demand any great intelligence. But it does demand the assumption that an involved and obscure style is not so much a sign of profundity of thought as of confusion of mind.

Thirdly, the sermon falls flat when the preacher has no sense of the dramatic. This is the place where one is tempted to say, "If he has it, fine; if he lacks it, nothing much can be done about it." The man who is not easily bored will probably never sense when he is boring others. The man who does not feel chills run up his spine when the right word is spoken or when an incident is observed that makes truth leap up and march may be an acceptable lecturer or writer. But he will never preach. Emily Dickinson said, "If I read a book and it makes my whole body so cold no fire can ever warm me, I know that is poetry. If I feel physically as if the top of my head were taken off, I know that is poetry. These are the only ways I know it. Is there any other way?" And, brethren, this is the only way you can know you have been listening to a real sermon. Truth is personal and truth is glimpsed in the midst of conflict. Great teachers can help a man understand that somewhat, but not much.

Of one thing I feel very sure. If the idea does not hit me with an excitement I cannot contain, it is not the Holy Spirit speaking. Furthermore, it can never be made exciting to my hearers, no matter how many cheap tricks and melodramatic tactics are employed. The drama has to be intrinsic, and discerning people will spot the pretender immediately. As a matter of fact, sincerity itself is dramatic. Timing is very important, and I have heard some fine illustrations fall flat as a statistical report because the preacher had no sense of when and how much. I have an increasing belief that the heart of drama is concreteness. Abstract preaching is always poor preaching.

Speaking with neither manuscript nor notes doubles the pleasure of the preacher and increases it tenfold for the congregation. When I read some fellow's article in a ministerial magazine arguing for the reading of sermons, I wonder if he has ever talked with his laymen. He may convince a few scholarly brothers who would rather be caught undressed than split an infinitive, but I never met a layman who would agree with him. Even an elementary understanding of communication will dispose of his arguments. I tried in vain to open an important pulpit for a sermon-reader, and the committee would not even take the time to go and hear him preach. A man may stubbornly hold to his custom of reading his sermons, but let him never deceive himself to the extent of believing that the people like it.

Anything that is done effectively and well always seems easy. This is true of all artists and craftsmen who know their jobs. Whenever I see a championship golf match on TV, it looks so smooth and simple that I wonder why we duffers make such a mess of it. A gushing woman came up after a sermon I preached on the "Lurline" en route to Honolulu and said, "My father preached just like you. He just stood up and talked." I wanted to say to her, "Lady, if that is true, he wasn't worth hearing." For to be free of manuscript will not lessen the work or demand less time for preparation. It may increase the work and it will certainly increase the strain of delivering a series of sermons if you have more than one a day. But it is worth it.

Every now and then somebody comes along to predict the end of preaching. True, we never have enough good preachers to go around. Many a thoughtful Protestant layman leaves the church feeling empty and frustrated, wondering if he would have been better off to read a book or listen to the radio. But the Reformation was born of great preaching, and every important rebirth of faith has been associated with the rediscovery of the centrality of preaching. For the spoken word is still the most powerful instrument for shaping society and affecting human lives. The church needs all sorts and conditions of men to do its work. But it will die without preachers, and a democracy cannot exist without free and flaming pulpits.

I have been preacher and teacher. Preaching is better. I have been preacher and writer. Preaching is better. I have been preacher and administrator. Preaching is better. When about once in a year I have a free Sunday, eleven o'clock finds me restless, nervous, and unhappy. I try to remind myself that a man needs a change of pace—to say nothing of his congregation. But there is a kind of panic takes over as I think what life would be without preaching. My friend W. E. Sangster of England wrote in the preface of his last book, shortly before he died: "I am a traveling preacher unable, by reason of sickness, either to travel or preach." I knew those were the saddest words any preacher could write.

CONSIDER
WITH ME . . .

AFRICA   In January of 1959, I made my third official episcopal
visit to a mission field—this time Africa. From the moment I looked
out on the red roofs of Lisbon on a bright winter morning, en route to
Monrovia, until I left Algiers two months later, it was one thrilling
experience after another. In many ways the African journey was the
most exciting trip I ever took. Two young preachers and one young
layman were with me much of the time, and out of our journey there
was born the Agricultural Aids Foundation to aid African farmers,
which in turn sparked the Congo Polytechnic Institute to train African
leaders. The financial support and leadership of Keith Smith, the
young layman on the trip, were chiefly responsible for launching both
of these Christian projects to serve the African people.

It is easy to be critical of the political and social conditions in Liberia,
but when you weigh all the factors involved, there are reasons. I do
think we could have helped to make this country more of a testimony
to the virtues of democracy and independence. But that is past and
we must grasp the opportunities of the present. There has been some
outstanding missionary work accomplished in relation to agriculture,
education, and health. Ganta, for example, is a Methodist station with
a hospital, a leper colony, a school, a mill, boy's and girl's hostels. The
road was a long and dusty day's journey from Monrovia north, but
Dr. Harley's hospitality and conversation at the end of the way were
refreshment and inspiration.

I liked the African people individually, and the children are among
the most attractive in the world. There is in their faces friendliness
and laughter, though many of them have little to laugh about. To see
the bright eyes and alert expression on the faces of the youngsters is

143

enough to win any man's heart. When President Tubman, an active Methodist layman, received me graciously, I remembered a friend's remark that whenever an African child in the jungle stubs his toe, President Tubman says "Ouch!" The African children are born with music in them and they harmonize about as soon as they talk. They could dance like professionals and the joy of life bursts forth from them like rivers in the wilderness.

We had a short time in Ghana and were most hospitably received by the British Methodists under the leadership of their British Chairman. Talk as you will about the baleful effects of colonialism, you cannot but admire much of what Great Britain did for her African colonies. There were roads, public buildings, a university, and a trained civil service when the British left. Indeed, I heard of one African government official who complained that his country had not had the advantages of colonial experience. Certainly freedom and independence are the ultimate rights of all peoples, but we should never forget how orderly has been the transfer of power to former British colonies compared with what happened in the Congo. At the Oslo Conference of World Methodism in the summer of 1961, I was present when Dr. F. C. F. Grant, president of the autonomous Methodist Church of Ghana, was introduced. How rapidly the people of Africa are assuming their position as equals in the councils of nations and of churches.

Though far apart geographically, the Portuguese colonies of Angola and Mozambique are similiar in spirit and political condition. Both are police states ruled by Dr. Salazar's dictatorship. Actually there was more opportunity for native Africans to attain citizenship and less racial prejudice under this regime than in some of the countries dominated by more liberal policies. But there was stamped on these lands a control that eyed every foreigner with suspicion. Our missionaries were harassed and our bishops have been under constant scrutiny. In a land desperately in need of medical help, we have been prevented for months and years from sending missionary doctors. Now the revolt is under way which the Portuguese meet with ruthless persecution and killing. I left both of those colonies with the same relief I felt on leaving Russia, for dictatorship from the right is no better than dictatorship from the left. Luanda looks like a smaller Lisbon and I have wondered if the Portuguese are not frightened that revolt in Luanda means revolt in Lisbon. It seems to me that there were some colonists in the eighteenth century who fired a shot heard round the world, and the revolutions started on that occasion are still going on today. Nor can you prevent the winds of freedom from blowing across colonial borders.

On February 7, we were met at Luluabourg by a young missionary originally from my conference, and we drove for the next three days more than a thousand miles through the heart of the Congo. From Léopoldville, a modern, beautiful city, it is quite a contrast to ride through the jungle over what we would call a fourth-rate road. Early in the morning a launch had brought us across the Congo River from Brazzaville to the Léopoldville airport, and now we were on our way into a country that had changed very little in hundreds of years. But scattered along that road we came to the missions of The Methodist Church with their centers of healing for bodies and spirits. I saw poverty, nakedness, disease, hunger, and even a corpse being carried to another village by two men. We went through cannibal country and places where the dreaded tsetse fly made it wise to close the windows in spite of the heat. Then, at the close of one day, we came to Kapanga with its hospital, its church, its schools, and its agricultural development.

The next day we arrived at Sandoa, the home base of my young agricultural missionary. Here, with his colleague, he was transforming a large farm into a demonstration of how the African farmers could feed themselves and raise their standard of living. The two missionaries were products of a very conservative seminary and a very liberal one. I asked them how they got along and one of them said, "Fine. We don't talk theology. We talk cars." Conservatism or liberalism is not decisive when two Christians are healing the sick, feeding the hungry, and preaching release to the captives.

Just before we arrived, a little girl had fallen from one of those tremendous anthills which rise over thirty feet. Her leg had been crushed and had to be amputated. I went to the government hospital to call on her and it almost broke my heart. She had been climbing the anthill because she was hungry and searching for ants to eat. I stood in the midst of the filth and stench of that government hospital and thought it would be better to die in the open than stay there very long. Then I prayed for her and her weeping parents and thought how that scene symbolized Africa with all its tragedy and all its need.

I went out to three or four villages with a missionary and the procedure was about the same in each one. We pounded on a piece of tin hanging in a tree and the people came from the fields, from their homes, from their work, to the church. They sang a hymn, we had a prayer and I preached briefly. The missionary told me he could have a service anytime, any day. I have never seen a more receptive people, eager to hear the gospel and anxious to hear more than one sermon if they could persuade the preacher. I met some of the most devoted and consecrated preachers and laymen in the world. In the midst of all the Congo turmoil since independence, I do not forget those wonderful Christians. And I do not forget the heroic leadership given during these desperate days by our bishops and our missionaries.

I preached one Sunday in our church in Elisabethville. Bishop Newell Booth, who acted as my interpreter, told me that the preacher who conducted the service was the son of a cannibal tribal chief. Now he was the pastor of a large congregation and a preacher of the gospel. Some of us have forgotten what Christianity has done during the past centuries and what it does today when it is set loose from our traditional and institutional chains. It is a strange thing that an American Christian should need to visit a simple, unsophisticated people to see his religion in its glory and power.

Southern Rhodesia is a beautiful country. Down around Old Umtali, which Cecil Rhodes gave to Bishop Hartzell for a mission, the country looks like a smaller, more widespread Yosemite Valley. Again I was impressed with the breadth of the mission program, which included printing, farming, education, child care, healing, and worship. I shall not forget a hundred or so children sitting under a tree on the slope of a hill singing "Heavenly Sunshine."

In Mozambique, we found the ruthless dictatorship of the Portuguese, aided by a Catholic archbishop who had accused the Protestants of being subversive. Beira had a luxury hotel where we stayed one night and found it nine-tenths empty. We were the only passengers on a small plane down the coast to Inhambane. There we were carried on the backs of men out to the sailing boat that took us across the bay, where we drove to Kambinie, an outstanding agricultural mission. A short way to the northeast was Jerusalem, which the Woman's Division operates with an educational program for girls as a part of the larger Gikuki station. It was like Hawaii, and along with the beauty of the moonlight on the water and the snoring of my companion, I was encouraged to stay awake much of the night. We stopped in Lourenço Marques to catch our breath and found its hotel and swimming pool sheer luxury after the long weeks of travel.

Johannesburg, South Africa, is another Chicago, and our work there is with miners who have come mostly from Mozambique. There for months they live in compounds without their families and toil in the gold mines for a pittance which takes care of their families for a year. I saw "apartheid" at work and I sat in one session of the treason trial of people who were guilty only of believing in human dignity and justice. I went down into a mine and talked with the manager. When I left after a week, it seemed to me that the old proverb, "Whom the gods would destroy, they first make mad," was being carried out before my eyes. For I did not talk to an intelligent man who did not confess to me off the record that the racial policy of the country could bring nothing but eventual disaster. What a terrible thing it is for a people to fall into the hands of a government dedicated to suicide rather than yield to common sense. For the end cannot be in doubt and one day there shall be taken away from the white man in South Africa his property and his life because a group of powerful fanatics chose death.

We made an overnight stop at Khartoum and then flew above the silver strip with green borders which is the Nile on its way to Alexandria through the vast and barren desert. We stayed in Cairo and saw the sights, which are many and varied. We went to Algiers via Rome and met some fine missionary leaders who work long and hard for meager results. I thought of the contrast between their work and the work in the Congo and decided it took even more devotion and courage to be a Christian among Moslems than among primitive tribes. Evangelism that is pleasing to God may be receiving a thousand people at the altar or baptizing a whole village. It may be also persistently and bravely bearing your witness for five years to win one convert.

Africa is changing so rapidly that no one will ever see it the same from year to year. The explosions on the "dark" continent are smashing the old but are not able to create the new. I venture to prophesy

147

that when the African people emerge into stable societies, they will remember a tremendous debt to Christian missionaries.

□ □ □

WRITING   I had four main ambitions which were: to marry the girl who became my wife; become a preacher; get a Ph.D.; and write a book. These were good ambitions, I think, for each one was the beginning of a great and endless adventure. The fellow who gets what he wants and then finds he does not want it has my sympathy. Life without ambition seems to me flat and unprofitable, but we need help in learning how to want the right things, which is not the least of the gifts of the gospel. So, after a number of false starts, my first book was published by Harpers in 1947.

I have no doubt but that much of the desire to write and be published is vanity, hence the success of the so-called "vanity" presses. As one of the editors of such a publishing firm put it, "Others may promise money, but we promise immortality." Pride fills the heart when, for the first time, you see your name underneath the title on the hard cover of a book. However, it becomes increasingly clear what Job meant when he wished "that mine adversary had written a book" (Job 31:35). This is the King James Version, for the more accurate rendering of the R.S.V. ruins my point. When you write it down, you can be quoted out of context and misinterpreted, often innocently but sometimes deliberately. I have a friend who seems to have memorized everything I ever wrote, and when I am holding forth eloquently, he covers me with confusion by saying, "But in one of your books you said this." By the time you explain what you meant there and what you mean here, the argument has been very effectively neutralized.

The greatest single reward that has come to me from my writing has been the number of friends it has brought me. Preachers and laymen from all over the country and abroad have written to me and greeted me in my wanderings. We are brought together by a book

148

whose ideas are the bridge we cross to meet one another. And I must say that if writing a few books had done nothing more than give me my friendships with editors and publishers, it would have been well worth all the effort.

I seldom meet a preacher who is not going to write a book "when he gets time." I listen to him with a sad feeling, for I know he will never write a book. Nobody ever gets time, and only when a man decides he will squeeze a few extra hours out of the day by sleeping less will he do any serious writing. It is a hard discipline, full of weariness and anguish. Many a time late at night or early in the morning when the words could not be found and the sentences limped, I cursed myself for a fool. What madness had ever tricked me into thinking I had anything to say? Emptiness is so much easier to disguise by talk. I learned you just have to keep going, for inspiration never meets a man more than halfway.

I am not competent to talk about literary men who write novels or plays or anything that demands full time. I am talking about the kind of writing that does not make any money but is done as a part of a man's ministry. Every now and then a young man wants me to give him the secret of being published. He wants an introduction to an editor or he wants me to read what he has written and tell him what is lacking. In the background of many a man's mind there is the conviction that if you know the right man or get the right endorsement, the trick is done. But so far as I am aware, there is no trick whatsoever.

I suspect that the publisher is in the same position as a bishop. Young preachers are sure that there is a plot to keep them from getting to the top tomorrow. It must be, they assume, that the bishop does not know talent when he sees it, or else he is committed to the theory that mediocrity is better for the church than excellence. But from where I sit the only question is, Where can the man be found who is able to do this job? The church is wide open to ability, and its search for leadership is sometimes desperate. So the publisher must be most anxious to discover new talent; and if the bulk of what comes from the presses is any criterion, he is not having much success in finding it.

Everybody seems to think he is a writer with better material than he finds in books. Probably everyone does have experiences which are significant, although what is important to one person may not be unique, as he thinks. And to write it effectively demands more hard work than most young men want to give. For writing has to be tight and sharp. The loose style that fits preaching will not do for the writer, and the first thing a man has to learn is that speaking and writing are two different disciplines. Send in fifteen or twenty sermons as they were delivered in the pulpit, and do not be surprised if they come back with a rejection slip. The first discovery to be made is that while repetition is a part of good preaching, it is the death of writing.

There is nothing to do but write and write and write until one has trimmed off the fat. The writing I admire aims inevitable words at the target with the directness of an arrow. It sounds so easy and re- laxed, but just try it! It is art, and we only begin to approach it after long and weary repetition. I am almost ready to say that good writing is just saying something important or interesting with the fewest words and the simplest words.

In the summer of 1945, I was invited to lecture and teach at Union Theological Seminary. This, I decided, was the time to begin writing in earnest, and a friend encouraged me to send the manuscript to the religious editor of Harpers. I remember the day I lunched with Eugene Exman, when he said casually that they would like to publish *His Word Through Preaching* and handed me a contract. Ah, that was peace and balm to the spirit. And when, some months later, we had a party at my church to celebrate my birth as an author, my cup over- flowed. Nothing quite compares with the publication of a fellow's first book.

It is a good thing to begin with a familiar theme you really care about. Preaching was the natural subject for me as I had been doing it, teaching it, and reading about it for years. Strong convictions give writing authority and interest. Nothing is more tasteless than writers who suffer from the disease of noncommitment, and perhaps this is the reason so many of us have difficulty in getting started. We have nothing to say that matters greatly to us personally.

If the first book goes fairly well—and being chosen by a book club is a great help—then a man may be requested to write. Like so many experiences in life it is either feast or famine, with a man starving to death one day and receiving ten different dinner invitations the next night. I remember talking with Professor Herbert Farmer about his writing and hearing him mention casually the requests he had received from editors. I thought that if any reputable publisher ever requested a book from me, that would be bliss indeed. When I was asked for a book of sermons by Harpers, I was so excited I promised more than I could easily fulfill. So I wrote *Have This Mind* in about one month in addition to doing the work of my church. But I was content.

A number of my books have been the result of lectureships which included the responsibility of publication. Thus the Peyton Lectures at S.M.U. became *The Lion and the Lamb;* the Slover Lectures at Southwestern University became *With Singleness of Heart;* the Beecher Lectures at Yale became *God's Good News;* the Mendenhall Lectures became *Who Speaks for God?;* while some of the material in *The Methodist Way of Life* was used in the Gray Lectures at Duke University. I had the privilege of editing *The Best of John Henry Jowett,* and was richly rewarded in reading everything he had written. I felt that I knew Jowett after that experience, and he is a great preacher to know.

My filing system consists of a drawer in my desk where I throw every illustration or scrap from my reading which strikes me as being usable as an illustration. When I am preparing a sermon I dig through the drawer until I find what I need. This is not efficient but it is a lot of fun and it seems to suit my purpose better than the filing systems my friends use and recommend.

One day when I returned from a trip east, my secretary had gathered some of the material into some semblance of order and asked me why it would not make a helpful book for preachers. It had never dawned on me, so I asked Harpers what they thought and they agreed it was worth a try. The result was *A Reader's Notebook* and six years later, *A Second Reader's Notebook.* It would seem that these would be easy books to produce, but the difficulty of tracking down all the sources nearly drove a young lady in the publisher's office frantic. Finally in desperation she put my name after the material she could not trace and I have been waiting ever since for a lawsuit or a bullet.

151

These are the only books with my name on them that I can recommend enthusiastically because they contain other men's material that appealed to me. Books of homiletical illustrations leave me cold and I can only hope that these *Notebooks* are stimulating and not nauseating.

I have found editors and publishers wonderful people. For one thing, they know their jobs and their suggestions are usually realistic and to the point. This is something hard for temperamental writers to accept: but ninty-nine times out of a hundred they are right. They know about the limitations which must be accepted for a book to be published at a profit, and they have had long experience in dealing with the kind of books that people will read. In more than fifteen years of writing, there has been only one instance in which I refused an editor's suggestion—and I still believe I was right. He wanted to shorten one of my books and wanted it done by a so-called professional. The sample he showed me was shorter all right, and for all I know better. But it was not mine, and until I deliberately employ a ghost writer, it must be my book or it cannot bear my name. I know one man who allowed his book to be rewritten and the result was stale writing with all the juice squeezed out of it. I take the same attitude toward my book that Touchstone took toward his chosen wife: "An ill-favoured thing, sir, but mine own" (*As You Like It,* V, 4).

Every preacher ought to write, though not always for publication. But to keep one's speech from verbosity and repetition, we need to practice the art of writing. Most professors of homiletics advise their students to write all their sermons and some—wrongly, I think— encourage young preachers to read their sermons the first few years of their ministry. I never wrote a sermon before it was preached, and though it would probably have improved my literary style, I am glad my sermons all reach the ear before they reach the eye. However, if I were starting over again, I would do more writing earlier, for the good of my soul.

An old professor once growled out irritably after reading another annual volume of sermons from a preacher not noted for his depth: "There ought to be a law forbidding any preacher to publish a book more than once in five years." I think of that as I look back and see some nineteen books published in sixteen years. It is too many and it has been hard work. I can only plead that I never did it for money, and there was always some diabolical deadline which I suppose I must have agreed to and then had to meet. Anyway, thanks to those who have read my books and have remained my friends. Or, as Hilaire Belloc put it,

> When I am dead, I hope it may be said:
> "His sins were scarlet, but his books were read."

□ □ □

AMERICA   In the autumn of 1935 I returned from my first visit to Europe and from my first opportunity to look at my own country from the outside. I knew then that too many things had been taken as a matter of course; and the greatness, the uniqueness, and the glory that is America came into new and sharper focus. I made a great number of speeches about Europe in those days and my conclusion was Henry van Dyke's famous lines:

> So it's home again, and home again, America for me!
> My heart is turning home again, and there I long to be,
> In the land of youth and freedom beyond the ocean bars,
> Where the air is full of sunlight and the flag is full of stars." [1]

Patriotism, like all virtues, is very hard to find in its pure state. So often it is a means to some ignoble end and a covering for some selfish ambition. Such common manifestations caused Samuel Johnson to define patriotism as the last refuge of a scoundrel. In his time too he must have observed unimportant persons seeking attention by accusing their betters of less than 100 per cent uncritical support of every government policy of the moment. He may have noticed men of questionable character trying to cover their shoddy dealings with the flag. But when a man desires to give his best to his country out of love and

[1] "America for Me." From *The Poems of Henry Van Dyke* (New York: Charles Scribner's Sons, 1911).

without thought of gain, his patriotism becomes sacred. He does not go about talking about it anymore than a man proclaims his love for his wife in the marketplace. Indeed, it is usually true that the more a man talks about it, the more likely we are to discover that his sentiment is phony.

I have visited four countries behind the Iron Curtain and I have been on all of the continents. My traveling has only increased my faith that America is "the last best hope on earth." It has never seemed to me, however, that my love of country gave me the right to be uncritical of it. One must point out to his brother, his family, or his church that there are some things we ought to do better. But let no outsider presume to express the same sentiments. I felt anger rise in me like a torrent when I overheard a loudmouthed Irish woman in Belfast say that Americans made her sick. Win or lose, prosper or fail, I am an American and all that I have belongs to America.

We are facing the most serious crisis of our history. We are confronted by a ruthless, tough foe who denies the faith by which we live and threatens to bury us. We have seen a Communist advance since the war that brings consternation to all who believe in God and the dignity of man. In the face of this advance, we seem to be curiously inept and confused. The time has come for some serious American soul-searching and hard, realistic thinking.

On June 10, 1961, the English historian Arnold J. Toynbee gave a speech at Colonial Williamsburg, Virginia. The occasion was the celebration of the 185th anniversary of the adoption of the Virginia Declaration of Rights, which has been called *The Prelude to Independence*. The eminent historical scholar called his speech "The Continuing Effect of the American Revolution," and among other things, he said:

I have the impression—and I think I am right—that contemporary America does not much like the contemporary British welfare state. Yet this twentieth-century semisocialist dispensation in Britain is one of the children of the eighteenth-century American Revolution. It often happens that one's children turn out differently from one's expectations and one's desires. Yet it is quite useless to try to disown an unwanted child. Paternity is a fact that has to be faced. By now, the eighteenth-century American shot has indeed been heard all 'round the world. The Revolution has become world-wide, and the Old World, as well as the New World, is swarming with the American Revolution's progeny. The Russian, Chinese, Egyptian, Congolese, and the Cuban revolutions display, unmistakably, their origins in the parent revolution in this country. And, at the moment, America's comment on this practical joke that destiny has played upon her seems to me to be fairly expressed in Queen Victoria's words: "We are not amused."

I have quoted this because I am sure it will shock the brethren on the far left and on the far right. But until we see through their propaganda, which is often subversion, we cannot be saved. This drive for freedom, equality, and opportunity which is manifest in a Congo village or in an Indian metropolis has the whole world in its hands. It does no good for Americans to self-righteously give thanks that we are not as other men or to view with alarm or to pretend that all this is a bad dream. It is not a dream at all and it is not about to go away. Maybe it will help us somewhat to realize that we started it and, while much of it from the viewpoint of experience is madness, still the flame of this worldwide revolution was kindled from our torch.

Now our situation makes it very difficult to sympathize with have-nots. For, to put it colloquially, we have it made and we would prefer just to settle down and enjoy our wealth in peace. Curiously enough, I saw our dilemma more clearly when I visited Russia in 1959. It is so much easier to give aggressive and inspiring leadership when there is so much to be done in a country. Russia seemed to me to be about where we were a hundred years ago, with a continent to explore and exploit. In some ways it is a psychological problem we face and some-what similiar to that of a middle-aged man caught in a world of adolescents. They have everything yet to win and he wants to be sure that he can preserve what he has won. The elderly revolutionist is not a common figure.

One sees this same thing in churches and it is a constant fight to keep something of the freshness of the vision, the excitement of the adventure, and the unselfish commitment which characterized the beginning. After Martin Luther had become embroiled in the tumult of the Reformation, he wrote: "Had I known all in advance, God would have been put to great trouble to bring me to it. I don't know whether now I could be so daring." The Christian church has great difficulty in keeping the Pentecostal fires burning, which is the reason God must continually baptize afresh men and movements within the church.

Look at it in your own life. My wife and I married while still in college, and I found it hard to understand why her parents were less than enthusiastic and why they were full of such gloomy forebodings and dire prophecies. Now I wonder how two sane people could have dared to launch forth on the sea of matrimony in such an unseaworthy ship. We were about as well prepared for the dangers ahead as the Congo was ready for independence. Yet we have lived together for more than thirty years now, which is a testimony to my wife's character. Getting married young was the smartest think I ever did. But let me confess something. When college students come to me for counseling about getting married, I urge caution in almost the same words my parents used when I was twenty.

Now caution and conservatism are fine traits, and America is right when she points out the facts of life to people who want freedom without the responsibility of discipline. But when conservatism becomes reactionary and caution turns into fear, we get hysterical and lose our sanity. This is our danger, and although thus far we have come through McCarthyism and I believe we shall survive John Birchism, one wonders how much energy we can afford to waste on these internal enemies. Will the time come when we lose all sense of mission and let our fears conquer our faith? Will communism conquer us without firing a shot? Could it be that mutual suspicion will poison our confidence and destroy our courage? It seems to me that we have been granted no built-in defenses against the inner complacency and blindness which have destroyed other societies.

There is always a great need for a responsible conservatism. We need to be warned about both the dangers of statism and the limitations of government spending as a solution to our economic problems. Indeed, the threat of the far right is never against the far left, for it actually drives middle-of-the-road people further left. Its danger is to a legitimate conservatism which we must depend on to keep our balance. We should not forget that the Nazis gave communism its opportunity to overrun half of Europe.

When we stop being forward-looking, we merely react to the enemy instead of outthinking and outmaneuvering him. Consider how much of our foreign policy has been mere reaction to Russia. If they start testing atomic weapons, then in two days we announce we will follow suit. If they give economic aid to underdeveloped sections of the world, we will promise more as a part of our cold-war strategy. Instead of being an act of good will, our generosity then becomes merely another weapon in the East-West conflict. The loss of the initiative is the most serious defeat we have suffered, and until we regain it we shall resemble an old hen clucking indignantly because her nest has been disturbed.

What must we do now? We must find a goal that will have all the appeal the frontier held for the pioneers. We must make the freedom of all men as exciting a purpose as freeing the southern slaves or making real the American domestic dream. It is a sad commentary on our loss of direction that we have to appoint a committee to determine our national goals again. It shows how lost we are and how our faith has diminished. This is really the most exciting time in all history for a nation with our power and our heritage. That we should sulk in our tent while the Communists fill the leadership vacuum we have left must make the fathers of the American Constitution groan in their graves.

We need to decide what kind of world we want and then adopt the policies which will bring it about. There is a good deal of risk involved here, as in all noble enterprises. But the very act of choosing will release the great powers of our spiritual resources and rekindle our faith. By dreaming again and opening our minds to a vision, we will allay our fears and silence the croakings of subversives of the left and the right. It is not strength we lack but courage and resolution. George Washington's words are as much to the point now as they were at the Constitutional Convention in 1787. He spoke of raising a standard to which the wise and honest could repair. "The event," he concluded, "is in the hands of God."

This is the responsibility and opportunity of the Christian church. Our failure has been a failure of nerve and a moral betrayal. We have preached ease and comfort when the times called for a Moses and a Paul. There is never any guarantee of victory, but in God's name let us face the future pointed toward life. Let us have no more of dedicating all our intelligence and our money to death. If we must make

157

sacrifices, let it not be to go underground and return to the caves from whence God has led us. Let a note on hope be sounded on the trumpets of the world and let a banner be lifted which promises an open society and freedom for persons. In a word, let this nation become the rallying center for all who are sick and tired of destruction and want to join a crusade to heal the sick, feed the hungry, and set men free.

I was on a train in Poland in the summer of 1961. We stopped at a station of a fairly large city, and an ice cream vendor tried to make a sale. As the train started to move he cried out something and waved. A friend who speaks Polish told me he had shouted: "Keep broadcasting." Our voice so often is low and squeaking. Let Madison Avenue use its skill to tell our message to the world instead of trying to sell more deodorants and cigarettes to an already glutted public. Let us use our skills of organization and production for something besides armament. We would be astounded at the allies we would find in all places, and I believe a sick world would rise from its bed and walk.

What a day this is for the Christian church! The battle is for faith, for the soul of man and the dignity of the individual. It is a contest of concern which is being waged, and it will decide whether a Christian nation can defeat an atheistic tryanny on these grounds. In a day when so many people cannot see who the real enemy is and what the real issue is, the church could make these matters clear.

We must not be sidelined or left behind while the world plunges on toward the abyss by following lying voices. In the words of Abraham Lincoln, we cannot escape history. As a Christian and an American, I have a goodly heritage. I have a promise to give to all mankind that will make the Communist propaganda sound like a cheap spieler at a carnival. As the spiritual father of my particular church one time put it: "The world is our parish."

JUST A
FEW WORDS
MORE ...

ECUMENICAL   I first became actively interested in the ecumenical movement during the Second World War. Of course the subject had been studied in seminary and the sin of Christians fighting one another instead of the world, the flesh, and the devil was plain enough. The great ecumenical conferences and the contributions, while not very specific, seemed to me important in creating a climate of mutual criticism and appreciation. With the world burning up, it was wonderful to read about Christians of all denominations and organizations forgetting their differences and standing together against the common foe. I think I am one of the few American pastors who read from cover to cover the published reports of the 1948 Amsterdam Conference.

Any Methodist finds it easy—almost inevitable—to be enthusiastic about the ecumenical movement. In the eighteenth century John Wesley said, "Is thy heart right, as my heart is with thine? Dost thou love and serve God? It is enough. I give thee the right hand of fellowship." He said also that the mark of a Methodist was not his opinions and that Methodists were willing to think and let think. We have had freedom of theological thought within the framework of our Articles of Religion, and it has been more than fifty years since we had a heresy trial. Even then the man was acquitted and it is impossible for me to imagine any minister or layman in our connection being brought to trial, unless he was obviously beyond the pale of Christianity.

This background makes it very difficult for me to understand the statement from the Central Committee of the World Council of Churches meeting in Toronto in 1950. The principle was adopted that "the member churches of the World Council of Churches do not necessarily recognize each other as true, healthy or complete churches, but they consider the relation of *other* churches to the Una Sancta as a question for mutual consideration." I can remember Bishop Oxman's impatience with the debate which ended with this statement when he related what had happened. For such a statement does not augur well for the formation of the One Great Church which some of the brethren talk about so eloquently. At least not in the near future!

At so many of the conferences I have attended, we spend much time in confessing our sin of division, our denominational pride, and our insistence that we are the one true church. I get a little weary of confessing this sin, which I do not think I am guilty of, and which I do not believe characterizes Methodism. I hasten to add that we have sins to confess which may be just as serious as these, and if there is any doubt about this, just read the *Christian Century*. But to confess sins just because others are confessing is hypocrisy. And so often the ones whose confessions of prideful division are most eloquent are the ones who will be the last to do anything about it.

There is something one is not supposed to say about the ecumenical movement, but I have found considerable pretense connected with it. I read in the paper a report of a stirring speech made by a church leader at New Delhi in the autumn of 1961. He rang the changes on the sins of our divisions and the need to become one. But it so happened that I had been in Poland the summer before where his church and mine were working together with a united witness in a Communist- and Catholic-dominated society. That is, they were working together until he came over and told his people that unless they stood entirely independent from the Methodists, they would not receive financial aid from their denomination in America. Since this came directly from one of this brother's colleagues in Warsaw, I have no reason to doubt it. From here on, I shall take his ecumenical pronouncements with less than respect.

Still, I believe in the ecumenical movement even when you must listen to the kind of lectures that made the late Archbishop Berggrav whisper to a neighbor, "'The Word became theology and did not dwell among us." I believe in it because it helps us to know one another and to love one another in spite of differences. I believe in it because my Christianity is partial and my church is not the only true

162

church. I need the challenge and tension of the Christian churches who have found truth about Christ and the gospel which has not found me. I want the wider Christian experience and vision which my own church cannot give to me alone.

There is a common treasury for all the churches which claim the Reformation heritage. Of course all Christians from the beginning have so much in common that it is a pity when the Roman Catholic church or the Orthodox church or anyone claims to be the sole possessor of the Christian faith. Such pride was so far from the Jesus of the New Testament that it demanded a Reformation to bring the church back to the straight way. Whenever any man calls his neighbor heretic unless he joins his church and does not deviate from his creed, the very heart of the gospel is denied. We must, therefore, inasmuch as lieth in us, unite with one another, love one another, appreciate one another. For the very differences give us more light to live by and bring us closer to our Lord.

We need one voice when we are facing the world and dealing with the social applications of our faith. We need a way to make our influence felt at one place and at a particular time. For on many questions the majority of Christians can find agreement easily, and in some matters there are strong minority groups who cut across denominational lines. The councils of churches in our communities ought to provide this service, and their lack of adequate support from the churches indicates that we have much to do on the local level. This poor support is sometimes due to lack of leadership and program on the part of councils, but mostly it is caused by the involvement of ministers and laymen in their own church affairs. Church executives must learn how to co-ordinate their efforts, and we must enlist more of our top laymen in the ecumenical affairs of our communities.

I have spent so many hours in dull ecumenical meetings, that when the National Council of Churches is attacked by fundamentalist groups and reactionary laymen, it rather lifts up my heart. You do not kick a dead horse, and for the National Council to be regarded as dangerous by these people is a great compliment to it. Believe me, it is not Christian success when all speak well of us, but probably it is time to call for the mortician. Whether it be Catholicism in South America, Orthodoxy in pre-Communist Russia, or a false prophet crying peace

163

when there is no peace from a Protestant pulpit in a prosperous suburb, our Lord is crucified again when churches becomes complacent. It is a fine thing when the ecumenical movement can stir things up and make the fellows bent on building larger barns uncomfortable. Amen!

However, when someone comes along to proclaim that we are duty bound to work for one Protestant organization, I get very uneasy. It is a cause for rejoicing when churches with similar backgrounds and polities decide to become one. But that we should strive to bring everybody under the same tent does not seem desirable to me. I am not impressed with bigness as the answer to the problem. I do not think huge organizations are necessarily the most effective. I cannot see how conflicting theological dogmas can be resolved without compromise, and when we move toward the lowest common denominator in any situation, we are likely to come up with dry bones.

The matter of organization is itself frightening when we contemplate a Protestant church of, say, twenty million. It would have to move toward authoritarianism unless it should be released from the laws governing human organizations. The Roman Catholic Church is authoritarian because it must be. We might try to run a huge ecclesiastical institution through committees, but that would create a bureaucracy that has very little to commend it as against the idea of a pope. Indeed, with two good friends I would like to launch a new movement called the Society for the Prevention of the Evil Effects of Devilish Bureaucracy on Methodism, or to give it a rather catchy title: SPEEDBOM. The difficulty is that I do not know how to go any further without making it a part of the disease it is supposed to cure.

Now the proponents of church union argue that it could be loose in its polity and everybody could be just as free as they are now. But if this were actually the case, there would be little sense in changing what we have. It would be better to strengthen our councils and perfect our means of co-operation. Every real union means that we all give up something. But if there are strong differences of opinion as to what is essential in the faith, I can hardly ask my fellow Christian to surrender his essential but allow me to keep mine. I would rather say that we shall both keep our essentials and work together in the faith which we hold in common.

As long as these plans are kept general, we assume that we can both have our cake and eat it. That is possible on neither church nor culinary levels. One of the very popular plans for church union of our time suggests that we ought to take care of every preacher as the Methodists do, and at the same time give freedom to each congregation to call its own minister. Let me tell you a secret. When a Methodist bishop reads the appointments at the Annual Conference, he knows that not every church would have accepted the man he is appointing if they could vote on him. Nor would every Methodist preacher go to the church he has been appointed to if he were not a man under orders. The church-union dreamers who promise that it is possible to have the best of all polities without giving up anything simply do not know what they are talking about.

I have a real concern lest we mistake what may be our strength for our weakness. When I was in seminary, the whole emphasis was on closing out our small churches and combining congregations to make one strong church. Since that time I have seen some of the results of those efforts. Hardly ever did it strengthen the church by leaving one where formerly there had been two. Of course there are places where this was wise strategy, but too often we lost both in membership and vitality. Two plus two does not always equal four in churches. Nor am I any more at ease when I consider the possibility of making our main Protestant denominations into one organization. Personally, even if I had the power, I would not cast the deciding vote to make all American Protestants Methodists. They could not stand it, and neither could we.

I do not know any place in the world where the Christian churches are more revelant or vital than in the United States. I know many places where our American activism is criticized and where empty churches with correct theology seem to be preferred over serving people. But in spite of all our sins—and they are many and serious—our American pluralism has produced churches with a continuous and restless Christian energy. We need to deepen our theological understandings, but not by becoming less active in proclaiming and demonstrating our Christian faith. The New Testament puts a great deal of emphasis on doing the truth.

Yet I would not close this on a negative note. Any movement toward closer co-operation or uniting churches will find me on its side. I hope that we may be saved from the excessive negativism of the brethren who spend most of their time bewailing our divisions and confessing the sin of parochialism. Let us rejoice in our unity and pray for those who are too exclusive. Let us strive for patience and understanding when we deal with those who substitute law for gospel. And, above all, let us not believe that nothing can be done until God has restored our divided Christendom. Let us rejoice in our present unity and freedom.

□ □ □

MEN   When I was having theological difficulties in the seminary, a professor told me to begin with personal relations. This was good, sound New Testament teaching, and it has helped me to help others in their doctrinal journeys. It is pleasant to look back over my life and think of the men whose lives have inspired me and strengthened my faith. Because I have had to fight bashfulness all my life, there have been opportunities to meet outstanding men which were passed by, to my regret. But in later years, my job has thrown me into contact with a number of great names and some of those experiences may be worth sharing.

In February of 1959, I spent two days with Dr. Albert Schweitzer at his hospital near Lambaréné, French Equatorial Africa. With three companions, we were met at the airport and taken upriver a few miles in a large canoe powered by lepers from the hospital. Dr. Schweitzer met us at the landing, and for the next two days we followed him about, ate with him, and had an hour with him alone before our departure. In the evening after dinner, he played the piano while we sang a hymn and then he led us in the Lord's Prayer. We talked with the nurses, the doctors, and the patients. I have seen few institutions which seemed to express so completely the spirit and influence of one man. Schweitzer runs the show.

I heard criticisms of the hospital from missionaries who felt that it was too much a one-man affair and who felt that Albert Schweitzer was lacking in awareness of the future needs of the Africans. They questioned whether proper attention had been given to the training of leadership to carry on after his death. Some have been critical of the rather primitive methods still employed. With the exception of the operating room, there was no electricity and in my room there was no running water. We found some outboard motors rusting away while the boats were hand propelled.

The visitor who expects an otherworldly saint whose gentleness encourages opposing opinions and whose "reverence for all life" puts animals on a human level will be disappointed. I saw Dr. Schweitzer angrily drive a dog off the porch and rebuke a lazy worker. Nobody else makes the decisions and even the doctors brought what seemed to me fairly routine matters to him. I can still see the old man (he was eighty-four) climbing the hills, agile as a goat, inspecting everything from the admittance of a patient to the repairing of a boat and giving the orders.

But all of this is unimportant. Here was a great man with a greatness which permeated the hospital and every person involved. It was something one could feel in the atmosphere. Even the animals appeared to be aware of his commanding presence, and those who worked there seemed to assume it was reward enough to be with Schweitzer. And why not? When one of the greatest men of our time turns his back on what our world calls success to devote his genius to the poor and forgotten, to be with him is one of the highest honors that can come to any man or woman. To see greatness shining through the human qualities of a man of action is about the most inspiring sight in the world.

One of the nurses told me about a time he was getting ready to attend the funeral service of an old priest in the Catholic mission. When he brought out his tie it was green with age and the cockroaches had chewed on it. She told him he could not possibly wear it but he said it was his only one and had been for thirty-two years. His father, said Dr. Schweitzer, had owned two ties but since one was always lost, he had decided one was enough. The nurse told him that in America there were men who owned one hundred ties. "One hundred ties," he murmured, "and only one neck."

I heard him discuss the growth of world law and restate his opinion of Jesus' teaching as an "interim ethic." He criticized the West in the nuclear bomb crisis, and spoke of the status of the laity. After answering a theological question, he asked with a smile: "Did I pass the examination?" "Don't cut me up like a cake," he said as we tried to separate his views on philosophy and theology. "I am just a simple human being."

He allowed us to take pictures and said drily that there was nothing like photography to teach patience. He saw us off and we watched the venerable, bent figure dressed in white, holding his sun helmet in his hand, until we were out of sight.

One of my friends was wise enough to bring pictures of Dr. Schweitzer with him and gave me one of the great man standing beside his interpreter and preaching. Inscribed on it are the words:

He comes to us as One unknown, without a name, as of old, by the lakeside, He came to those men who knew Him not. He speaks to us the same word: "Follow thou me!" and sets us to the tasks which He has to fulfil for our time. He commands. And to those who obey Him, whether they be wise or simple, He will reveal Himself in the toils, the conflicts, the sufferings which they shall pass through in His fellowship, and, as an ineffable mystery, they shall learn in their own experience Who He is.[1]

Beneath this quotation from his writings, Dr. Schweitzer wrote: *A Bishop Gerald Kennedy avec mes bonnes pensées, Lambaréné 5. février 1959. Albert Schweitzer.* This is one of my most precious possessions.

I met another great man in the autumn of 1951. We were in Japan and Dr. Kagawa invited us to call. I never met a man whose mind seemed to encompass more interests and whose curiosity seemed more alive. He talked about geology and oyster culture. He discussed the possibility of importing Swiss cattle to Japan's mountains since they were adapted to high country. He outlined the Christian strategy for defeating communism in Japan. He reported on his evangelistic campaigns and what he had learned about winning people to Christ. His eyes were almost gone, his voice was husky and rasping, and his English was hard to understand. But there was a shining quality in

[1] Schweitzer, *The Quest of the Historical Jesus* (New York: The Macmillan Company, 1910).

his face and I knew it was my privilege to sit in the presence of a saint.

In November of 1957, my wife and I had the privilege of going around the world in thirty days with Bishop and Mrs. Bromley Oxnam. I never enjoyed a trip more, largely because of the joy of being with such very dear friends. Certainly when the history of The Methodist Church in the United States is written, his name will be one of the brightest in the twentieth century. He liked to travel fast and not stay in any one place very long. So do I. He was never late but always ahead of time. That is for me. Because of his prominence, the doors to government leaders were wide open to us, and I met a number of political leaders.

In Seoul I preached to President Syngman Rhee and spent an hour with him the next day. I had the impression of a tough old warrior whose mind had become set in a pattern of steel. He would no longer change it, no matter what new situations might rise. In Taipei, we met Madame Chiang Kai-shek, and for sheer charm, she will be forever at the top of my list. It would not be gentlemanly to speculate on her age, but she had the vitality and vivacity of a teen-ager. It is my judgment that beautiful women who have nothing but their beauty are pretty pale and insipid beside the women who have found a cause.

I shall not forget the tall Ecumenical Patriarch Athenagoras in Istanbul. Bishop Oxnam and I rode to the service on Sunday morning in his Cadillac while our wives followed in a cab, because women cannot ride in his car. It was most satisfying to live even for thirty minutes in a man's world. What a friend America has in this man, and how gracious and generous he was to us. There had been riots, the destruction of Christian property, and the wind of persecution seemed to be rising. I asked him why they did not leave and he answered: "There have been Greeks in the city now called Istanbul for twenty-five centuries and there have been Christians in this city for twenty centuries. How could we leave?" I saw in him Christian leadership at its bravest and best.

But it was in India that the government leaders impressed me the most. Nehru seemed to be both a statesman and a practical politician. I must confess that seldom has a man disappointed me more than he did with his agnostic attitude toward God. We were with him an hour one evening and there was no doubt but that he is both able and intelligent, but he is not religious, although he followed Gandhi's method of nonviolence because it worked. We have so many Christians who accept nonviolence as a theory but do not actually believe that it will work. I think it has been a good thing that India and its prime minister have stood between the East and the West to point out matters which we would rather ignore. I felt strongly that he is on the side of democracy and that his country is a test of whether an underdeveloped country can rise within a democratic framework. I think his attitude toward Christian missions has often been prejudiced and the Goa affair was most unfortunate.

It is an unusual thing to have as a nation's vice president a great philosopher. But such is Radhakrishnan. He talks fluently and beautifully with that Oxonian accent that makes even the commonplace sound cultured and important. He spoke of a policy he was advocating, and I asked him if it was practical in the present world situation. He said that such a question was not the one to raise. "God says to us," he said, "to bring him our failures if they are the right ones." I thought this was a most unusual thing for a politician to say and it seemed to me that we could use more men with such an attitude.

I never knew a more dedicated man than W. E. Sangster of the British Methodist Church. We spent a Sunday evening in his home after I had preached in Central Hall, London, in 1951. A press interview was set up for him in my office in Los Angeles a few years after that, and I listened with delight as he preached the gospel to the newspapermen while answering their questions. For Sangster, preaching or witnessing was as natural as breathing; and when you find such a man, you see the ministry in power.

I have never cared much for most of the "celebrities" I have met. My work has brought me face to face with some movie stars, some entertainers, and some stage personalities. Too often they are very ordinary persons who, through some quirk of publicity or some not-great talent, have become widely known. Most of them seem to sense that they have to make it now or it will be too late. They must not be ignored at any cost, and this leads to a frantic, almost hysterical desire to be seen and admired. It must be terrifying to them when, after a comparatively short time, they are forgotten. It is bad enough for a bishop. There are a few exceptions and it is a great joy to meet a person who does not take the popularity very seriously. Best of all is to meet a celebrity who has real character and a sense of moral values, but there are not many of them.

Politicians always make me uneasy. They are under greater temptation than I am, and if they try to please everybody and see each decision in the light of the next election, I do not find it in my heart to judge them harshly. We place them in this position and we judge them on the basis of our agreements rather than according to their character. The marvel is not that sometimes they do not vote according to their convictions, but that so often they do. Anyone who has to deal with the general public soon learns to respect a man whose professional life depends on it and who still keeps his integrity and his courage. I have known two or three such men and they have been inspirations to me. And this even when I disagreed with them.

The most exciting thing that happens to me is to meet a good man. Usually he is not an international figure and often he is not known beyond a rather small circle. I have found him in my congregations and in my community relations. I remember the saints I have known who shamed my own poor life. They have done more to make God real to me than anything in nature. They make the publicity addicts and the notoriety seekers about as attractive as ten cents' worth of cold potatoes.

EDUCATION   Away back in 1945, I was asked to review a book before a teachers' group in Lincoln, Nebraska. I chose Jacques Barzun's *Teacher in America.* I never forgot the opening sentence: "Education is indeed the dullest of subjects and I intend to say as little about it as I can." A book that began with that point of view had to be good. Teachers are wonderful, and teaching is exciting and important. But I never had a course in education that did not bore me to death, and I never heard a lecture on the subject that ever got out of the realm of abstraction. Education and teaching is the contrast between reading Calvin's *Institutes* and hearing a great preacher, or the difference between reading a blueprint and seeing a temple. The nineteenth-century writer T. L. Peacock wrote a classic word: "The bore of all bores was the third. His subject had no beginning, middle, nor end. It was education. Never was such a journey through the desert of the mind, the Great Sahara of intellect. The very recollection makes me thirsty."

I have sometimes wondered why this subject, which is so important to all of us, cannot be made lively. It is partly because of the jargon connected with it, which is nearly always academic. The language is dead and educators are overly fond of five-syllable words. They would rather be intellectually unassailable than understood, and to get immediately to the point is considered gauche. You can usually tell an educator by his talk.

Then, theories of any kind are hardly ever able to make the blood flow faster unless a fellow is an expert who can picture the implications. Theories of human behavior are fine, but when my neighbor's dog barks all night, it gets to my emotions. I appreciate the debate between theologians on original sin, but I had not taught a class of ten-year-old boys for ten minutes when I knew which side I was on.

In my time, I have seen theories of education ebb and flow like theology. One day it is all one thing and the next day it has swung in another direction. I do not doubt but that all these theories have had their value and all their proponents have made contributions. But the older I grow, the more I question that any theory can contain the whole truth. Certainly this is the case in theology, and since education also deals with whole persons, it can never sum up the truth in a single proposition. There are too many exceptions. Any idea carried to an extreme becomes false since all our convictions need the tensions of their opposites. I suppose that to some extent this is the position of the existentialists, and this far at least I am with them.

Dorothy Day, who has done so much for the poor and disinherited and who edits the *Catholic Worker,* put this whole matter very clearly in her autobiography, *The Long Loneliness.* She wrote:

Once a priest said to us that no one gets up in the pulpit without promulgating a heresy. He was joking, of course, but what I suppose he meant was that truth was so pure, so holy, that it was hard to emphasize one aspect of the truth without underestimating another, that we did not see things as a whole, but in part, through a glass darkly, as St. Paul said.

In my seminary years, John Dewey was all the rage and we even tried to make Christian thought conform to his ideas. The fact that Dewey was not a supporter of the Christian faith made no difference. Those were the days when we were trying to fit religious doctrines into contemporary thought patterns. After this had gone on for a time one of my friends, who was president of a theological seminary, told me that his main requirement for a director of religious education was a fellow who had had a case of Dewey and gotten over it.

We have been through an educational teaching that has been called "progressive." This is a very broad term and means many things to different people. But it often affirmed the wrongness of external discipline and advocated freedom for children to follow their own bent or interest. It was assumed that unless a child wanted to study, it would do him no good. Their personalities were sure ·to be twisted and damaged beyond repair if they were coerced by adults in the school or at home. There must be some exhibits of this process which bore out the theory of its excellence. But I have seen too many spoiled children in "progressive" homes which made it agony to visit with the parents and aroused in every visitor a resolution never to return. I believe children can turn out well without making life unbearable for others.

I believe, and this cannot be proved, that much of our modern juvenile delinquency springs from progressive education. It is seldom that I pick up a newspaper without a story of some shocking vandalism or violence on the part of teen-agers. Of course there have always been such youngsters in our midst, but to have whole sections of cities terrorized is surely something new. The thing that impresses me with these young gangsters is that there seems no place to take hold in dealing with their lawlessness. You cannot say that it is wrong, for they seem never to have been taught that there is a difference between right and wrong. You cannot appeal to con-

173

science, for this seems to have atrophied through neglect. It seems to me that something essential has been left out of their education.

I quite agree that until a young person has said yes to a proposition freely and without pressure, no real decision has been made. But this does not mean that to cut young life loose from standards and rules will bring this about. A friend of mine told me of a kindergarten playground that was fenced in because of the proximity of a busy street. A new director with new ideas ordered the fence taken down under the theory that children should not be fenced in. But to his surprise, they huddled over to one side of the playground and seemed curiously uneasy. Finally they asked if the fence could not be replaced because it made them feel safe. I do not think that rules and disciplines are automatically bad.

There is a certain amount of experimenting every child has to do for himself. No adult can tell him what will happen in a way to convince him. He has to blunder through his own experiments, which is the main reason the human race does not progress any faster. Too much experience has to be repeated. But now and again someone stands for something that makes its appeal to a young person. There is something in a person's life, in his conversation, in his interests, that makes a boy say, "I would like to be like him." When that happens, a great decision is made and a life has gained a sense of direction.

I had a good many teachers I did not wish to become like at all. But there were a few whose minds gained my immediate respect and whose personalities won my admiration. I have seen this happen to children from rich and cultured homes and I have seen it happen to children from the slums. It is the creation of an image which removes a good many temptations and eliminates much wandering. It has happened in one-room schools and it happens in the most modern and well-equipped schools of the cities. Once a life has been captured by an idea, discipline will take care of itself. But I believe that this is more likely to happen to those living within the framework of moral laws.

Education is no good unless it leads to a discovery of one's own abilities and limitations. In his essay on "Self-Reliance" Emerson said,

There is a time in every man's education when he arrives at the conviction that envy is ignorance; that imitation is suicide; that he must take himself for better for worse as his portion; that though the wide universe is full of good, no kernel of nourishing corn can come to him but through his toil bestowed on that plot of ground which is given to him to till.

This holds true for the above-average child as well as for the below-normal one. It is the beginning of pride in a sense, but it is also the birth of humility. For it comes to us that others will excel us in many ways, but there is a particular contribution we are expected to make. This is individualism in the best sense and it is essential for a democracy.

I was appointed by the governor to the Califorina State Board of Education in 1961. It has been an enjoyable duty and a rare privilege. But we deal with the mechanics for the most part; and while it is necessary work, it does not get to the heart of it. What kind of people are teaching and what is the quality of their characters? What is the content of the courses? For we have gone too far in assuming that techniques are the main things while the material studied is unimportant. The churches made the same mistake, and for a time we had methods but not much biblical content. Happily, that is no longer the case in most of our denominations.

My own education, such as it is, has come to me from many sources and from many people. I never have talked to a man who did not have something to teach me. I have tried to sound out a man about his job and learn something of its scope and purpose. There have been times when an unschooled man has opened my eyes to wonderful things I never learned in college. If we can succeed in developing curiosity in our children rather than stifling it, we shall have accomplished much. Education enlarges our capacity for wonder and appreciation if it is done properly—which is one of the main reasons secular education without any touch of religion fails to accomplish its purpose.

I still believe that everyone needs a liberal arts base. If we are to do more than merely survive, we need much more than technicians, engineers, and scientists. We need men aware of their culture and with the ability to appreciate the things of the spirit and heart as well as of the mind. A democracy cannot live without the bulk of

175

its citizens equipped to resist the hysterias which sweep over us every now and then. The rich industrialists or the narrow professional brethren are often so naïve. With no knowledge of art, history, sociology, and international affairs, they are a gold mine to the crusaders of the far right or of the far left. They are also a constant threat to themselves and their country.

I do not expect we shall ever arrive finally at a perfect system of public education. It will always be an arena of conflicting theories and practices. One day we are to learn everything from reading the *Great Books*. Another day we are to learn it all from experience, whatever that means. But I am cheered with the high quality of the people who give their lives to education. With few exceptions, they are men and women of broad vision, liberal spirits, and faithful devotion to their calling. They are among the best citizens of the community and a bulwark against tyranny.

I believe in the American public-school system; and anyone who tries to weaken it or destroy it is, in my judgment, subversive. I am not enthusiastic about parochial schools, and even less so when their proponents try to get their hands in the public till. I want to raise the standards of teaching and I hope for a deeper appreciation of teachers. It is a great and essential profession and to have it harassed by self-appointed champions of narrow orthodoxy should bring every decent American to its support. For what we are going to be tomorrow is being decided in large part by what is going on in the classrooms of our public schools today.

I must confess that I become very uneasy with all the talk about mechanical contraptions to speed up and enlarge our teaching processes. There are machines which will do everything from teaching the subject to grading the papers; television systems which will increase a teacher's range a thousandfold. But is education merely the imparting of facts and is there to be no regard for the teacher and the student as persons? After all, survival is not the only issue—although it is an ultimate one. Yet we had better pay some mind to the question of whether we are worth survival. And that will be determined not through mechanical methods, but by the miracle of personality. God, we must remember, usually comes to people through persons. In education, as in Christianity, it is "I and Thou."

176

YOU HAVE BEEN
VERY PATIENT...

TRAVEL   My job involves much travel, which I do not look forward to as a rule. If my wife and I get a few days in the summer for a holiday, we do not go anywhere. We stay home. Yet she tells me that if suddenly there were no more journeys to take, I would get mighty weary of the same place. She is nearly always right, and when I begin to feel sorry for myself because another long and tedious trip faces me, her words cheer me. Actually it is a privilege to see other places both at home and abroad, but I begin most trips counting the days until I can return.

Traveling for the minister is a necessity. From the time I took my first tour of Europe on a bicycle, it has been clear to me that a man who is called to preach the gospel must know more than his own land and people. There is simply no substitute for saying, "I was there." Most of the narrow fanatics have never seen the people or the countries they rave against with such passion. Traveling in Russia, for example, gave me an even greater horror of the Communist tyranny, but it gave me a deep respect for the Russian people. Indeed, the people who seem to like Americans best are Russians and Australians. It is important that we learn how to hate an evil system and love its victims. It seems a little incongruous to me that so many Americans speak with such venom about Red China when our state department will not allow any American to travel there. I have read two books on the internal situation of China—one by a Frenchman and one by an Englishman—and they give some impressions you never get from our press. I am always a little suspicious of the experts who have never known at first hand what they pontificate about.

179

The bane of the traveler is the fellow who wants to show him everything. This is the experience of some of the bishops who have visited mission fields, though it does not always happen. But now and then you are taken in charge by a guide who wants to show you every classroom in the school, every nook in the church, and even the storeroom in the hospital. When at the end of the day you are glassy-eyed and your knees buckle, you swear that you will never get caught in such a situation again. But you always do.

I found myself in such a trap in Africa one time, and thought there must be a way of escape. I suggested to my host that rather than look at any more institutions I would prefer to see some farms since we wanted to form a foundation to aid African farmers. He said that was fine, and we would start an hour earlier in the morning and go through a couple of schools before taking off for the farms. All I accomplished was a longer day.

But I am churlish to object to these occasional situations. Our missionaries are wonderful hosts and they put up with a lot. We take them from their regular work and we impose upon them in a hundred different ways. They open their homes and their hearts, and a Methodist soon discovers that he has friends all over the world.

Traveling with a purpose—and that is the only kind worth doing—is hard work. In the old days, when men went by ship, there was a chance to catch your breath going and coming. Bishop Matthew Simpson, for example, took seven months for a visitation to California and Oregon in 1854. But today we fly to save time and we are caught up in the preaching, the meetings, and the social occasions immediately. I may fulfill my last obligation in Brazil, or in Australia, or in Malaya, and in a few hours I am facing the piled-up desk and all the accumulated responsibilities of the Los Angeles Area. The crowning discouragement is when some well-meaning but ignorant brother greets you with "Did you have a pleasant vacation?"

The Methodist Church is a world church and it can only remain so if its leadership knows something about the world. That is why bishops take an official journey to some mission field every quadrennium. But in addition there are places where a man needs to travel if he is to bring the chaotic picture of our time into any sort of perspective. There have been few, if any, years since 1948 that have not found me out of the country for about a month. Traveling is like reading, in that the more you do, the less time you need to spend in one place. You can spot similarities, differences, and trends if you have a wide base of experience. For example, it helped me a great deal to understand something about Poland in the summer of 1961, because I had been in Russia, Czechoslovakia, East Germany, and Yugoslavia. While South American nations are not all alike, they have certain great cultural similarities, and a man may draw some tentative conclusions about Argentina if he has been to Peru and Chile. The main thing is not to have some preconceived idea which blinds you to reality, or to assume that what is not done the American way is automatically inferior.

I have a friend in Arizona who has been always on the conservative side. His conversation was a reflection of right-wing politics and pre–twentieth-century economics. If he had any opinions about international affairs, they were parochial. Then, about seven years ago, he began taking long summer trips all over the world. He is a social man and a friendly one. He met all sorts and conditions of men and talked with business and political leaders. The last time we were together, I was astounded at his grasp of issues and his opinions. It was no longer an echo of the superpatriot, but extremely broad, liberal, and inquiring. I asked him if he talked that way to other people, and he confessed sheepishly that he did not. "Most of my friends would think I have gone crazy," he said, "but this is the way I feel." And I was astounded at what travel had done to a man's thinking that had been set in a narrowly orthodox pattern.

Too many of my impressions of a country are likely to be colored by my physical comfort or lack of it. When you are weary with a long day's work, it means a great deal to have a comfortable hotel room and good food in the evening. It is difficult to appreciate a land where the sun beats down with over one hundred degree intensity, and the air is full of dust and the food covered with flies. It is easy for an American visitor to do much harm in such situations by showing a disgust with conditions which are far from his own standard of living. It is amazing to think back on how much influence the weather had on my judgments. To see a city in a driving rain and then to see it on a clear autumn day is like seeing two different

181

cities. Gradually, after considerable travel, one begins to take these external conditions into account and to be less influenced by them.

I have learned the most while traveling in non-Christian lands with different cultures from my own. More than a decade ago I visited Japan for the first time and my admiration for the artistry of the people and their sense of beauty has increased with every visit. Who can forget the river trip in Bangkok or walking through Singapore at night! There is a fascination about India and a curious pull in Korea. The Orient has so much to give us, and the courtesies which have been heaped on us from that part of the world are among our precious possessions. A long weekend in Istanbul was made memorable by the hospitality and the fascination of Moslem culture. I shall not forget St. Sophia.

There are places where the sense of history is so overpowering that you are transported to the past. A few years ago we were in Palestine, and to be in the land of the Bible was such an experience that I was filled with excitement day after day. "If I forget thee, O Jerusalem . . . ." Rome has the ability to carry a modern man back to the first centuries. Athens is the Olympian gods but more than that, it is Paul preaching on Mars Hill. One gets something of this reality of history in cities like London and Paris, and even more in Edinburgh. We do not sense so much of it in the United States, although there are New England towns which have it. Williamsburg is fine, but it is too artificial to create an authentic sense of the historical. Americans have too much interest in material progress to either preserve or appreciate their past properly.

The great cities of South America are beautiful. I remember Rio de Janeiro, Buenos Aires, Santiago, Montevideo, and Lima. But I felt more at home in Mexico City, perhaps because it is nearer to the spirit of an American city. I am too impatient with the corrupt and unstable governments of our Catholic-dominated southern neighbors. When one thinks of all the natural resources and riches of those countries which remain to this day undeveloped, one wonders what is the real contrast between North and South America. I think it is primarily the religious cultures and I have come to believe that no stable and free democracy is possible without a strong strain of Reformation spirit. John Fischer, writing about Yugoslavia in

Harper's Magazine for September, 1961, listed four necessities for democracies and the first two were: an Anglo-Saxon political tradition; a strong infusion of Protestantism, with its toleration of pluralism. I agree with him.

When it comes to sheer travel enjoyment, there is no place like Europe. The countryside is lovely, the cities are comfortable, the roads are good, and the hotels are excellent. Here are our beginnings, and we return with joy to England and the Magna Carta, France and the French Revolution, Italy and the Renaissance, Germany and the Reformation, Switzerland and independence, Scandinavia and cleanliness—which John Wesley said is next to godliness. We shall not forget a journey in our own car one autumn which took us to Spain along the French and Italian Rivieras and finally back to Germany by way of Austria. One gets more help and courtesy in villages or in cities than he expects, for foreigners are not to be despised but helped.

I have wanted to be in every main section of the world and so we went to Australia, New Zealand, and the South Seas in the winter and spring of 1962. It was a preaching mission, and whatever else may characterize the brethren from Down Under, they keep their visitors busy. I found that Americans are immensely popular in that part of the world and that Australian Methodism is more like the American Methodist Church than is any other Methodism in the world. There are few, if any, more thrilling missionary stories than what the church has done in Fiji and Tonga. I believe that Australia, New Zealand, and the United States are destined to come closer together in every way, including the separate branches of the Methodist Church. Australia could become the Protestant base from which our missionary attack on the Orient shall be made. It is, for instance, a shorter distance from Perth to Djakarta than it is from Los Angeles to Honolulu.

The changes in the world are apparent to the man who travels. Africa is changing so rapidly that it is no longer the same continent it was in 1958. Japan has become so westernized in a decade that it is not the same country. I have been told that Cuba is something different—and from our standpoint worse—from what it was when I visited there in 1956. India moves more slowly, but it is following great plans for new development. A fellow needs to see Israel every other year to keep up with it. All of this seems more real and exciting when you were there on some past occasion and can compare it with the present.

Do you remember that wonderful beginning of Lawrence Sterne's *A Sentimental Journey?*

"—They order, said I, this matter better in France.—You have been in France? said my gentleman, turning quick upon me with the most civil triumph in the world.—Strange! quoth I, debating the matter with myself, that one and twenty miles' sailing, for 'tis absolutely no further from Dover to Calais, should give a man these rights."

And there it is. Nothing punctures a proclamation like the simple question, Were you there? And nothing gives a greater personal satisfaction than to reply, Yes, I was there and I saw it.

□ □ □

PREJUDICES   I should say that the things I want to mention here are not really "unreasonable predilections" as the dictionary defines prejudice. But they are personal attitudes which carry with them tinges of emotion and, according to some of my friends, they are dark places in my mind. Of course they are wrong, but every man is entitled to his opinion.

Let me begin with the current craze for psychiatric analysis. Granted there is very much mental sickness among us and such cases do need professional help. But while sitting under bo trees and contemplating our navels is bad enough, we do something much worse. We pay experts to help us contemplate our egos. No one can do that very long without becoming convinced that his mental life is in pretty bad shape. There was a great Teacher who told us that "whoever would save his life will lose it" (Mark 8:35). A generation with too much luxury, too much leisure, and too little purpose tries to escape boredom and meaninglessness by looking inward. The results are not happy.

I wish I could observe some cases where people have been healed of their frustrations and redirected to healthy living by the psychological counselors who swarm about us. There are a few people who do not seem to have been harmed by their treatments, but there are a number whose condition is worse than before. I shudder when a preacher tells me his wife is going to a psychiatrist, for too often she comes out of it convinced that she must have a career of her own. Or she believes that the church has made unreasonable demands upon her and she must assert herself even if it means wrecking her husband's ministry.

An excessive introspection is not healthy, and the whole psychological jargon encourages us to make it the main aim of living. I heard the other day that a well-known psychiatrist had announced that even when people think they are happy, they may be mistaken. As a newspaper columnist remarked, this does not increase one's confidence in the profession. We seem bent on finding names for all our mental difficulties and then we assume that this is the same as healing them.

I think every minister needs to learn all he can about psychology and psychiatry. He needs to be a skilled person in counseling with people who have troubles. But learning techniques will never be a substitute for the quality of his own life. Indeed, it is getting so that if a man cannot make a go of his own marriage or his own ministry, he joins the staff of a counseling service where he can tell others how to do what he could not do himself. I keep wondering what kind of religion it is that has so little power in time of trouble that a man runs away from it to find his answer in the secular field.

Today everything must be organized and formalized. A fellow does not decide to take off some weight by walking instead of riding in his car or by simply cutting down on the amount of food he eats. He must join a gymnasium or buy some reducing machinery. Ministers can no longer do their pastoral work as a part of their larger ministry, but they must hire professional counselors for their staff who in turn will refer the "clients" to another professional. Parents are constantly on the lookout to find some community service which will entertain or educate their children. It seems to be decided that family responsibility should be reduced to the minimum. It is this spirit and not "creeping socialism" that increases the power of the state and decreases individual ability and importance.

I have a great prejudice against superpatriots. I am always unhappy and embarrassed when a fellow wraps himself in the flag publicly and proclaims how much more he loves his country than anybody else. Usually he is sick with an unhealthy longing for recognition. Unable to achieve anything positively, he takes the negative road of hate and suspicion to get attention. His devotion is mainly verbal, and when you analyze what he has done for the country, as a rule it is mighty little. Such fellows have never understood America, and the Bill of Rights was drawn up to protect us from their bigotries. The Founding Fathers were not nearly so worried over the dangers of free speech or radical ideas as they were over the subversions of these self-appointed champions of orthodoxy.

I suppose the truth is that I do not like what may be called "the fundamentalist mind." I do not like it in religion, in politics, in economics, or in education. The good, honest conservative has my respect, but there is something about the championing of a static past that makes people mean. They usually put material values over human ones, and they would rather protect their profits than feed the hungry. The extreme left usually strikes me as silly and irresponsible, but the extreme right seems to me dangerously evil.

Have you ever noticed how certain jobs seem to turn people toward arrogancy and rudeness? Of course there are many exceptions, but are there not more than a proper share of hotel clerks who have forgotten ordinary pleasantness and courtesy? If the hotel is full it is especially noticeable. They can spend more time going through a file without looking up while the guests wait for their keys or their mail. I remember a friend of mine saying to one of these clerks, "Do you want to take care of this for me or must I call for the manager?" That got a little action. It is so wonderful to come into a hotel weary from a long journey and receive a pleasant welcome and a courteous assistance. If I were a hotel manager I would try to help these people see that their jobs are really a ministry.

Speaking of hotels, do you know how hard it is to get a quiet

186

night's sleep in one of them? Especially in this country! They have connecting doors or they have television sets and radios which the people next door play as if they were deaf. I am waiting for a hotel chain to spring up across the nation without anything to offer but a good night's quiet rest. I would venture that they could eliminate a lot of expensive extras and be full every night.

I do not like bureaucrats. I mean I do not like the bureaucratic minds which try to appear important by acting superior to the people they are supposed to serve. You are likely to find some of them in post offices and they are nearly always present at the city hall and the county courthouse. Maybe civil service does it to them by making them secure. Perhaps the work is dull and this is the way they keep their self-respect. More and more these people appear in department stores. You go to buy something and three of them are over in a corner gossiping. Do they come over to wait on you? They do not. You have to break up the chitchat and get dirty looks for being so inconsiderate.

More people are using toothpicks in public and chewing gum. I am willing to concede that a toothpick is a handy gadget under some circumstances, but is there anything more crude than picking your teeth in a restaurant? And when it comes to chewing gum, I am a fanatic. I conducted a funeral one time and a lady came down to view the corpse with tears streaming down her cheeks and chewing gum in her mouth at the same time. It made even her sorrow cheap. In other countries Americans are supposed to be gum chewers and they pass out the stuff as the typical American gift. Some gift! We seem to be rapidly approaching the time when our countrymen will resemble nothing quite so much as cud-chewing cattle. Can we be saved or is it already too late? Chewing gum is not quite so bad as licking your knife in public, but almost. It is in the same category with the off-key whistles in offices and public places.

What gets into drivers who stay on the inside lanes of our highways and drive far below the speed limit? Why won't they get over into the slow lane and let the people who are going somewhere be on their way? They always remind me of those people in our churches who have no intention of going forward and spend their energy in blocking other people who still believe that the kingdom of God is as a man traveling. You can talk all you like about speed and its dangers, but these irritating, thoughtless, slightly stupid drivers push men to madness. In desperation to get around them, decent people take dangerous chances—which does not make it right, but it does explain where the fault lies. If America's highway patrols would concentrate on giving tickets to the slow ones blocking normal traffic, our highways would resemble smooth, flowing lines instead of snarled up booby traps.

I do not like alibiing preachers. We have a large number of brethren who are never to blame for anything and can find at least three people at fault when anything goes wrong with their ministries. It is always the official board, or the lay leader, or the president of the Woman's Society, or the district superintendent or the bishop. Sometimes I expect it *is* another's fault, but when the same thing happens in pastorate after pastorate, one begins to suspect that the guilt is closer home. I have known men who could have been saved if just once they had been able to say, "It was my fault." God sends us defeats to teach us something, but if we refuse to learn, we turn into poor weaklings who would rather alibi and die than accept the responsibility and live.

What makes a person a bore and why are so many of them good people? The little girl had this in mind when she prayed: "O God, make all the bad people good and make all the good people nice." What a dull and deadly thing some of us make out of virtue, until we cry out for some exciting sinner to relieve the monotony. The minute the bore enters the room, the joy is gone and we sneak away as soon as possible. Some of these fellows must have made a lifetime study of how to make conversation agony and their words leaden.

I have tried to analyze this trait and, while some conclusions have been formed, the worst offenders have been endowed with supernatural and hence undefinable powers to be dull. The man who goes into too many details when telling a story can make any tale sound as if it were told by an idiot. Who cares whether it was Wednesday or Thursday, 1909 or 1910, or whether it happened to Aunt Ethel or Cousin Sophy? Get on with it, man, and tell us the point, if there is one. Bores always load their speech with clichés until

188

they sound like a television drama. There is never a fresh expression or a heretical hint. They love old proverbs and will drag them in whether they fit or not. They labor the obvious and while their listeners have already seen the conclusion and found it disappointing, they plod on step by weary step until a fellow considers murder. The less they know about a subject, the more they will interrupt to make their asinine remarks. And they always mistake generalities for wisdom.

I am not happy around people with no sense of humor. Have you noticed this grievous lack in extremists—and perhaps this is the main reason they become extremists. The Communist countries I have visited seemed to be gray, without much sparkle. They are so deadly serious about everything and nobody laughs at the pomposities. The rightist cannot recognize a satire and ponderously attacks it as if it were to be taken literally. I suppose they are more to be pitied than censured but they are so unconsciously ridiculous that I have the feeling they are not quite human. Believe me, there is no surer sign that your cause is evil and your way is wrong than to feel hate supplanting love and to suffer the loss of joy.

I do not like the contemporary emphasis on happiness as the goal of life. A complete release from tension would make a man fall apart, and if we concentrate on finding happiness, we shall never come close to it. I remember that one of my happiest times was when I had the flu a few years ago and stayed in bed for two days. I was in no pain and all my commitments had been canceled for forty-eight hours. I would read until I was tired and then take a nap. But this was only a lull and it would be a fit way of life only for a vegetable. I got back into the tensions, the struggles, the weariness, the irritations, with great joy. Happiness is going somewhere with all your might, not sitting around complaining about the trials or feeling sorry for yourself.

I am always uneasy around people who are too self-consciously spiritual or pious. One of my colleagues once said that in all his life he had met only one authentic saint, and she did not know it. Some people are always having devotions, which is all right if they would not insist that everybody else join with them. I sat on a mountainside early one morning watching the miracle of dawn. One of these devotional brothers said we ought to have a prayer service, and coward that I was, I closed my eyes while he droned on for three minutes. I wanted to keep my eyes open and watch the sun lighten the eastern sky. It did not seem to me to be a place for words, and maybe because of a guilt complex at my unreligious resentment, I have tried to avoid that brother ever since. I thank God that the New Testament does not lead us down the murky, sanctimonious trails, but up into the sunlight of the presence of One who makes us sure that this is our Father's world.

□ □ □

MEMORIES   It seems to me that memory is one of the most difficult things to understand. Why does a man remember this but forget that? For if your memory is anything like mine, you do not always remember what the world regards as the big, important things but you cannot forget some trivial affair which, so far as you can see, had no decisive significance. I am sure that the will has something to do with this and, to some extent at least, a man may decide what he will forget and what he will remember. Herein lies the responsibility of parents and of culture. We must be aided in remembering the right things. How well Israel understood this and Moses' words to the people have always moved me:

Hear, O Israel: The Lord our God is one Lord; and you shall love the Lord your God with all your heart, and with all your soul, and with all your might. And these words which I command you this day shall be upon your heart; and you shall teach them diligently to your children, and shall talk of them when you sit in your house, and when you walk by the way, and when you lie down, and when you rise. And you shall bind them as a sign upon your hand, and they shall be as frontlets between your eyes. And you shall write them on the doorposts of your house and on your gates.

—Deut. 6:4-9

190

None of this nonsense about letting children grow up without being influenced by their parents until they are old enough to make their own decisions!

The memories of childhood are vagrant and undisciplined. I remember riding with my father in a horse and buggy somewhere in northern Michigan. He was going to preach in another village and he tied the back wheels with a chain when we came to a steep downgrade. It must have happened during my fourth year. I remember being urged by parents of a friend to stay for supper although I had been told to be home at a certain time. I yielded to the invitation and came home late to receive a spanking. My explanation was not accepted, and it was the only time in the first four years of my life that I can remember questioning the justice of my punishment. I remember my father losing his temper when the cat walked across his freshly painted kitchen floor. There must have been more important things than these which happened to me in those days so long ago, but that is about all that stayed with me.

When I was five years old, we lived in a small town north of Fresno, California, and somebody gave me a rabbit. Somehow he got out of his cage and was never found. My mood was a curious mixture of shame and sorrow—shame at letting him get away and sorrow that he was gone. I played baseball in the fifth grade and was captain of the team which we called the Americans. I remember that the night before a game I agonized over the batting lineup, changing it a dozen times with some wild hope that if it were right we would win.

My memories of adolescence and teen-agedom tend to blur and become a general impression of misery and wild hope. But when I am dealing with the mercurial temperament and illogical behavior of young people caught in this period, I remember my own reactions and can sympathize. The quarrel with the girl, the defeat in the contest, the inhuman discipline of parents, the tyranny of teachers—all come back to me in the lives of young people about me. Perhaps this is the chief value of memories, and if adults could remember there would be less of a gulf between the generations.

I graduated a number of times and each one became less important and exciting. The one I remember the best was from the eighth grade. What a night that was! Our parents were there, we all wore the class colors—the girls had them in the ribbons around their corsages, and the boys had them in some kind of boutonniere on our coats. We sang the school song and some songs we learned just for the occasion. I made a short speech which I thought went rather well. We had a party afterward and stayed up until 11:30. Parents with cars took the boys and their dates home, but we had no car and I walked a young lady a few doors and then walked home through the darkness, dreaming of the future.

I remember the first date I had with the girl who became my wife. It was the evening I closed my junior year in high school and became a senior. She was just right and there was never anyone else for me after that night, although we had our quarrels and went our separate ways from time to time. This is a mysterious matter and utterly illogical. Why not someone else, and why are we so sure that this particular relationship was settled from the foundations of the world? I never was able to take lightly the despair and broken hearts caused by teen-agers' love affairs, even though in later perspective they may appear absurd. By the same token, I have no desire to walk that path again. But if you have found the right wife, the most important matter has been settled successfully.

The time I lost a public-speaking contest in high school still stirs me with the remembrance of unendurable misery and hopelessness. This was due largely to the fear that if I could not win against that kind of competition, how was I ever to become the greatest preacher in the world? Yet the memory of my consecration as a bishop in The Methodist Church is so vague that I could not tell you what happened or anything definite about the order of service. Strange that one event is so sharp and clear while the other is lost in mist.

There have been some great experiences of nature, though my weakness is that they were hardly ever ends in themselves. Always there was a wondering of how these visions could be shaped for homiletical use. I stood one day with a friend on the top of Half Dome in the Yosemite Valley. I felt the first twinge of nature mysticism and all my sophomoric doubts about God disintegrated. I knew in that moment that there is a more-than-human power in the world that is personal and friendly. The only other time I can recall that same feeling was my first look into the thrilling depths of the

Grand Canyon. As an English novelist once put it, if the Colorado River carved it out, you are sure that God gave the Colorado River its instructions.

There is a waterfall and a pool in the Connecticut hills where as a student preacher I swam with some young parishioners. It still seems to me one of the most beautiful sights in the world, more wonderful in my memory than Niagara or Victoria. There is a cave in New Zealand called Waitoma. With my wife and a preacher friend, we were pulled quietly along in a boat while the glowworms on the ceiling were like a vision of the stars at close range. I am convinced that what Nature says to me is never so dependent on its magnificence as on my own mood and what is in my heart at the moment.

In my last pastorate in Lincoln, Nebraska, there developed a winter Saturday afternoon and evening ritual. About 4 P.M. I would arrive home, put on old clothes, and go for a long walk with my wife. We walked through an empty park and followed a path among the bare trees, often through the snow. Two hours later, we returned to a dinner which always included some special cinnamon rolls, steaks, little green onions and chocolate pudding. Then I went to bed early and read a book, usually a detective novel, until I was sleepy. Let my more spiritually minded critics make the most of it, but this was the most satisfactory preparation for Sunday I ever found. Ah, those wonderful Saturday evenings!

I wish that my musical memories were on a higher plane. There were times when we went to New York and got standing room at the Met and then drove home to our Connecticut village the same night. I was going to learn to like opera if it killed me—and it nearly did. I remember a Stokowski concert in San Francisco when my brother-in-law and I were locked out on the fire escape where we had retreated for some fresh air. Someone finally heard him yelling, "Leopold, let us in," but I cannot remember the music.

There was a night in Boston when my wife and I went to a musical comedy which was trying out before hitting New York. We did not expect much but we were in a good mood and we left the theater humming the tunes of *New Girl in Town*. It was not the greatest show written, but in our memories, it was a great night. I will never forget the night I first heard "Seventy-Six Trombones" in

193

The Music Man. I remember the singing of the old hymn "Let the Lower Lights Be Burning" in the Broadway show *Say Darling.*

In 1962 I was on a preaching mission in the South Sea Islands, New Zealand, and Australia. Because I was preaching two or three times a day and seven days a week, my mind was always on the next sermon. One morning in Melbourne, the maid came to clean the room and we had learned that if we did not take her when we could get her, we never saw her again all day. So I walked down the hall and found a chair near the elevators. I was irritated and impatient every time someone stopped near me to talk or the elevator stopped at my floor. Then, to make everything worse, someone started to play a violin in a nearby room. I got up and walked back to see how the room service was progressing. The maid was not finished but she said brightly, "Have you been listening to Yehudi Menuhin?" "Huh?" I asked like a dolt. "Why," said the maid, "he has a room near where you were sitting and he usually practices about this time every morning." I went back, sat down and said to myself, "Isn't this fine? I am listening to one of the world's great violinists. And it's free and I am his only listener. How many people have ever had such a private concert?" My irritation evaporated and my impatience was suddenly gone. Mr. Menuhin, I still remember you.

My first high-school debate and my first sermon in the pulpit of the First Methodist Church in Modesto, California, are not forgotten. I remember the first time I preached in Riverside Church, New York, and at the Sunday Evening Club in Orchestra Hall, Chicago. There are a number of pulpits not to be forgotten, such as Central Hall, London; First Presbyterian Church, Pasadena; Duke, Harvard, Cornell, Chicago University chapels; the Admiral's flagship of the Sixth Fleet; First Methodist Church, Evanston. There have been some great conferences I have been privileged to address.

To remember the good, the noble, the true and forget the evil, the false, the betrayal is one of the main ways to happiness. It is not so easy, and for ordinary mortals it is not completely possible. Yet I am sure that we can all learn to develop this skill to a larger extent than we usually admit. I have made a little progress along this road and I hope for even more in the future. It is not wise to dwell on humiliation, defeat, bitterness, or slander. I have known preachers who carried a burden that finally broke them which could have been unloaded had they been able to exercise more control over their memories. Some things ought not to be put into words and some things ought not to be dwelt upon. There is nothing sentimental or unrealistic in Paul's admonition: "Finally, brethren, whatever is true, whatever is honorable, whatever is just, whatever is pure, whatever is lovely, whatever is gracious, if there is any excellence, if there is anything worthy of praise, think about these things" (Phil. 4:8).

The older I grow, the more I thank God for my memories. What wonderful experiences the Lord has given me and how the long travels have stored up treasures in my mind. I have known great men and good men. I have seen some strange and wonderful sights. William Penn said in his eulogy of Isaac Pennington, "As the Memory of the Just is Blessed, so to me there seems a Blessing upon those that have a right Remembrance of them." And to that I say Amen!

THIS
AND I'M THROUGH...

FINALLY   One of the occupational hazards of the episcopacy is mail. It comes to my desk like snowflakes in a blizzard. Mimeographed material is delivered to me by the ton and promotional propaganda has given the janitor in my building a lame back. But one can deal with such trivia in a hurry. It is the letters which must be answered that make a man's nerves quiver. Or the manuscripts the sender assumes I am dying to read.

There are the crackpot letters written by pencil on ruled paper, either threatening destruction of the church or promising it salvation through the revelation of miraculous vision. There are the hate letters attacking a man or a cause and dripping anti-Semitism or exuding the fascist stink. There are the sincere but stupid solutions to the world's problems from people too ignorant to know how ridiculous they are. And a man throws them into the wastebasket and wonders how democracy can possibly work since all these people have votes even as presidents of corporations, banks, and universities.

I am amazed at the number of people who have all the answers. I wish I was as sure of anything as they are of everything. I get discouraged by the cocksure people who tell me that they represent 95 per cent of the congregation and 80 per cent of the members of The Methodist Church. They would do well to find ten other people willing to be seen with them in a public place. A man's opinion is to be trusted according to his humility, for if any man has reduced the complicated issues of our time to some simple proposition, you can be sure you are listening to a fool.

Yet nearly all my mail is sensible, fair, honest, and encouraging. My faith in the people has grown stronger with the years and I believe

199

that the democratic way is not only the best but the most secure. I am impressed by the way church bodies like the Methodist General Conference hardly ever yield to hysteria or panic and usually arrive at sensible decisions. I do not share the fear which assails some of my brethren when McCarthy or Welch or Browder seem to ride high for a time. Give them enough rope, and one morning the gallows they have built for all nonconformists are occupied by the builders. A free society will veer sometimes to the left and sometimes to the right. But the people will not be fooled for long and God seems to have provided enough people with enough common sense to keep us within safe distance of the center. Such is my faith.

I do not mean to imply that this will happen automatically without any effort or sacrifice on our part. Freedom is a constant fight, and tyranny from the left and the right ever waits to exploit our complacency or our cowardice. But there is an unconquerable love of liberty and a respect for persons in mankind which is the guarantee of our hope. We lose battles but we never lose the campaigns.

When on a preaching mission in Australia in early 1962, I had a number of seminars with preachers. I was astounded at the number of times I was asked if America was going fascist. The word itself shocked me, for while it seems proper when applied to parties in some countries, it seems utterly foreign to my native land. But these questioners were referring to newspaper and magazine stories about the revival of the far right and they were worried. My reply was always that America would not go fascist any more than it would go communist. Why? Because of the Christian church. Every church, every minister and priest, every congregation, is an attack on communism and a bulwark against Marxism. By the same token, the Christian churches are a society's defense against subversion from the right. For the Christian message is freedom and the Christian faith is rooted in the worth of each man's life. It is, in a word, a constant proclamation of the right to dissent and an insistence that nonconformity is strength. The heritage of the Reformation is the nation's chief guarantee that democracy is here to stay.

I believe in the moral law. Indeed, my experience has been so clear that I have not the slightest doubt that what a man sows he reaps, and no man gets away with anything. Every time I have tried to cut a corner, I have paid for it so obviously that only that horrid impediment called sin prevents me from being morally perfect. I know it in my mind, but I continue to fall victim to the temptation of compromise. It seems to me quite obvious that the moral law holds for individuals, for nations, for societies, and for civilizations. History has many exceptions to most of our explanations and theories, but it speaks with the clearest voice and is utterly consistent in the long run with the belief in moral law.

It has taken me a long time to see this, and I marvel that it did not become plainer earlier. It was easy to be careless about financial matters when I was in college, and I encounter men sixty years of age who never got over that weakness. When I see young ministers foolishly flaunting the Ten Commandments or more modern refinements of these ancient principles, my first impulse is to deal with them harshly. Then I remember the times when I was as bad or worse, only they are caught and I was not. I talk with them with the sad feeling that they regard me as a moralizing old fool who never faced what they face and whose virtue is mainly verbal. Indeed, to live morally is not so much a virtue anyway, as a matter of common sense. But it is the foundation on which the religious life—the good life—has to rest.

Looking back over the years, I cannot feel that personal credit is due me for escaping the moral destruction which has overtaken some of my contemporaries. Can any man think of those hairbreadth escapes he has experienced and believe that he has saved himself? Was his life more valuable or more noble than the ones destroyed? No, of course not. It was, as John Newton put it, the amazing grace of God which brought him through. I should be much better than I am but I think how much worse my poor life could have been, and I can only confess in wonder and awe the marvelous things which Jesus Christ does for the least promising of men.

When I was preparing for the ministry and even in the early days of the ministry, I was ill at ease to be known as a minister. I kept it quiet whenever possible and it was embarrassing to have some well-meaning person refer to me as *Reverend* in a strange crowd. I spent four months in Europe one time and never breathed a word to a soul about my profession. But the older I grow, the prouder

I am to be known as a Methodist preacher. I am even glad to be known as a Methodist bishop. For my affection for the church has increased every year and I envy no man his position. I wish that my father could have been alive when the Western Jurisdiction elected me a bishop in 1948. He would rather have seen me in that position than president of the United States. I share his judgment.

I am more puzzled than shocked at the way some men invest their lives. I look with pity on all those who exploit some legitimate racket and become millionaires. Who needs so much money and who can sink so low that his life means no more than making profits? Does no light of eternity ever penetrate such minds and is there no intimation that God has more than this to give? Not everyone can or should be a minister, but every man ought to see his work or his profession as his contribution to the kingdom of God. I do not think any man deserves to be a minister, and I can only conclude that the ministry is a striking example of how God uses the weak things to confound the mighty, and the foolish things to shame the wise.

The church seems too broad and simple for many of the intellectuals. I once had a letter complaining that my preaching should have been more intellectual. I was talking to some people one day when a man asked me if I preached a children's sermon in the morning worship service. Before I could reply, one of my parishioners said, "He doesn't need to. His regular sermon is so simple that the children can understand it." There was a time when such talk would have distressed me. I wanted people to be impressed by my academic training and my degrees. It makes me smile when the young Ph.D. makes sure that those letters always appear after his name. I was once the same. Now it pleases me most when a ten-year-old boy or girl comes up at the close of the service and gravely thanks me for the sermon. The late Pat McConnell of Boston once described himself as "just a simple, Bible-lovin' Christian." Me too.

I do not despise scholarship and intelligence. May the good Lord save us from equating ignorance with piety. But Jesus spoke in such manner that the common people heard him gladly while the Gospels make the philosophers seem verbose and involved. I do not think we understand what we are talking about unless we can say it plainly. So the church will have none of this putting certain people on higher levels than others, but it insists that the gospel will be the bread of life for all men. Each will take from it as he is able and some of the best educated will be able to pick up only a few crumbs. I want to preach to all the people and I have no desire to minister to a class or to just one age group. As a matter of fact those who have become such preachers have, in my judgment, lost their power.

The future just now looks rather dark. The difficulty of the present and the threat of distruction have become clichés, which is too bad. The situation is serious enough, but to hear so many speakers reminding us of it day in and day out tends to make trite what is terrible and urgent. So much of this speaking helps to create the attitudes which it bewails. If we can succeed in making men hopeless, we shall only hasten the destruction we fear.

It is a time for great affirmations and for the preaching of faith in God. I admire the courage of the secularists who are trying to say some hopeful word in the face of the threat of complete extinction. But their words have a hollow sound, for they are fooling no one but themselves. There is nothing they can appeal to which offers hope, and their optimism is the whistling of a small boy walking through a cemetery on a moonless night. It would be just as well for them to keep silent rather than to pretend to a confidence they cannot establish.

The Christian cannot believe in annihilation. He cannot believe it in regard to himself and, in spite of the horrors of our time, he cannot believe in it in regard to his world. He knows the possibilities as well as any man, but he knows also the God who so loved the world that he gave his Son to redeem it. When Eugene Vale gave the manuscript of his great novel *The Thirteenth Apostle* to the University of Southern California Library, he said, "From the Greek tragedy to the latest novel, only that work can survive which inspires in us the thrill of recognizing man's grandeur." I prefer to believe in man's potential status as a child of God and to look at the future through that truth.

When I was twenty years old, my father was in his early fifties. I regarded him as an old man whose temptations were all past and whose dreams must be dominated by yesterday. Yet in my own experience each new decade—after the shock of the birthday is over—has become as exciting and promising as the one before. Indeed, in some ways life seems to grow more stimulating with every passing year.

I remember the first time it came to me that one day I must die. It must have been about my thirty-fifth year when suddenly I realized that, like all my fathers before me, death was my destiny. It is a shattering moment and for the man without faith in God, it can be disastrous. One does not become aware of an increasing loss of his contemporaries without serious self-examination. But I have growing assurance that dying will not be greatly different from entering another decade. And I believe it will not be a limiting experience but an expanding one. Debates on immortality interest me very little because I know that my thoughts on the subject are shaped by my experience of God in Jesus Christ. It is there I find the essential clue to this life, and the next.

LASTLY   Now, brethren, forgive me for taking so much time. When a man gets on his feet to announce that he has nothing to add, he is likely to stay there too long. Still, it is a fine thing to be able to discuss matters of mutual concern with one's peers. It is exhilarating to speak frankly and personally with those too polite to walk out. Do you remember Ezekiel's words? "And he said to me, 'Son of man, stand upon your feet, and I will speak with you.'" (2:1.) Which leads me to conclude that there are only two positions for a man to assume in the presence of God. One is on his knees praying, "God, be merciful to me a sinner." And the other is on his feet saying, "Here am I. Send me!"